1950s Childhood

1950s Childhood

Spangles, Tiddlywinks and *The Clitheroe Kid*

DEREK TAIT

AMBERLEY

First published 2013

Amberley Publishing
The Hill, Stroud
Gloucestershire, GL5 4EP

www.amberley-books.com

British Library Cataloguing in Publication Data.
A catalogue record for this book is available from the British Library.

ISBN 978 1 4456 0977 5

Typeset in 10pt on 12pt Sabon.
Typesetting and Origination by Amberley Publishing.
Printed in the UK.

Contents

Contents

1

At Home

Just five years after the Second World War, 1950 began, with food and clothing rationing still in place. Clement Attlee was Prime Minister and George VI was on the throne. At home, hardly any families had a television set, there was no central heating or hot water and many had an outside toilet at the bottom of the yard or back garden.

All houses were heated by a coal fire in the front room, and if you wanted a bath, there would be a tin one filled with boiled water heated on the stove. The tin bath would be placed in front of the fire, as that was the warmest place in the house. Small children would be washed in the kitchen sink, which was deep and made of porcelain. Baths in the winter were dreaded because everywhere in the house would be so cold.

Many houses had no hot water. There was no central heating and homes had single-glazed, draughty windows. Ice would form on the insides of the windows. Heavy curtains helped to keep out the draughts.

Doors were left unlocked and neighbours would pop in, unannounced. People talked more, knew their neighbours and looked out for each other. There was no thought of being attacked or burgled in your own home.

Families crammed into the kitchen, which was probably the warmest room in the house with the heat from the range. Many people used their front room just for special occasions and it was kept tidy for this purpose. Many were hardly ever used because of this.

Mothers would stay at home while fathers went out to work, earning an average wage of £100 a year (in 1950), although many people were paid a lot less than this. Few families had a washing machine and most laundry would be done by hand. Only a very small percentage of the population had telephones, televisions or fridges. At the beginning of the 1950s, washing was done using a washing board and a bar of soap. Clothes would then be put through a mangle to squeeze out excess water before being hung out on a line in the fresh air to dry. Housework at this time dominated the life of a mother, and all week would be spent washing, shopping, cleaning and making meals. With the lack of a fridge, food was kept in a larder (or pantry) and bought daily from the corner shop. Some food kept well, but perishable food had to be eaten quite quickly. The meat safe in the pantry had wire mesh over it to keep away flies and other pests such as mice. Children were regularly sent on errands to the local shop to get extra items used for meals and the shopkeeper would get to know them well. Items such as half a loaf or half an onion could be bought, as well as all the other food and essentials needed to keep a household going. With the lack of a fridge, milk was kept in a bucket of water to keep it from going off.

At the beginning of the 1950s, a housewife's work was never done, with endless washing, ironing, cooking and cleaning. Activities not even thought of nowadays, like scrubbing the front step to the house, were seen as something to be proud of, or ashamed of if it wasn't done. Comments like 'Look at the state of her front step!' seem ridiculous nowadays.

Most families also didn't have their own car.

With no television, the only sounds in the house would come from clocks ticking loudly in the background or Dad rustling the pages of the paper as he read the day's news.

Entertainment came from the radio, the gramophone player or from reading books.

Board games were also very popular. Children played on the streets with no fear of danger. There were fewer cars and many didn't pass along the backstreets anyway. Bomb sites provided the perfect playing ground for children, who would re-enact scenes from war films and pretend to 'machine-gun' their friends with toy guns or, occasionally, real guns found on bomb sites or left over from the war.

Although it was a new decade, the war still played a big part in people's lives and there were shortages of everything.

Rationing meant that foods such as meat, cheese, butter and sugar were all in short supply. Sweets were also rationed.

Older people were treated with respect and called 'Mr', 'Mrs', 'Sir' or 'Miss'. There were policemen regularly on the beat, and any misdemeanour from kids would result in a 'clip round the ear'.

Rationing came to an end on 4 July 1954 and restrictions were lifted on the sale of meat and bacon. Food rationing had started on 8 January 1940, just four months after the start of the Second World War.

Most mothers knitted and children were kept warm with home-made jumpers, hats, scarves and mittens. Even swimsuits were knitted for those special trips to the seaside or local baths. The click-clack of knitting needles could be constantly heard around the house, as mums, grans and aunties all made clothing for the family, including the many children.

A typical beginning to a day for a boy or girl in the early 1950s would start with them waking up in a cold bedroom, perhaps with frost on the inside of the windows if it was winter. The bed would be covered by a sheet and a blanket, with maybe a hot-water bottle to keep warm. Many houses still didn't have bathrooms and a wash may have taken place in the kitchen sink with, if you were lucky, warm water boiled on the stove.

Some houses without bathrooms would have a bath in the kitchen; it would be covered and used as a work surface when not in use as a bath. Some households didn't have proper bathrooms until the mid-1960s. If the household was lucky enough to have a bathroom, it was very different from a bathroom of today. Because most houses were heated by a coal fire, the only places that were warm in the house would be in the front room or the kitchen, if the stove was on. There was no central heating, or other form of heating, so the bathroom was a very cold place, especially in severe winters. Often, the water would freeze overnight in the U-bend of the sink or bath. There was no toilet in the bathroom; this was in a separate area outside at the back of the house. Because of this, many people had chamber pots, which they kept under their beds and emptied in the morning. Toilet paper, called Izal Germicide, resembled slippery tracing paper and was of little use for the purpose required. It came in cardboard boxes that fitted into a metal holder. Some families cut up squares of old newspapers, which were hung in the outside privy to be used instead of the shiny alternative. A trip for a child to the outside toilet once it had got dark could be a daunting experience. Meeting mice, rats, countless spiders or toads wasn't an uncommon experience.

Bedrooms, at the beginning of the 1950s, would only be a place to sleep and would consist of utility furniture, including a bed with scratchy army blankets, and a wardrobe. Many floors would have been uncarpeted and rooms would have been unheated, with meagre contents and draughty windows. There would be no posters of pop stars or film stars and very little other decoration.

Mum would have the children's clothes ironed ready for school in the morning. For boys, this consisted of shorts, socks, shirt and knitted jumper. Many boys wore short trousers until they left school at fifteen. They were part of the uniform whether it was summer or winter. Shorts were often grey flannel, and fell to just above the knees. Long socks for school were expected to be pulled up, and many mums made their children wear elastic garters to keep them up, which is probably where the phrase 'Pull your socks up!' came from.

Once dressed, children would have their first meal of the day. Breakfast consisted of a soft-boiled egg with buttered toast cut into soldiers to dip in the egg.

Cereals were also available and milk would be delivered early to the door by the local milkman. Like the postman and other people delivering to the house, the milkman would be smartly dressed and wearing a uniform. Many dads would either be rushing their breakfast while having a quick look at the newspaper or would have already left the house to travel to work by bus or train. In the early 1950s, as mentioned earlier, few families would have had their own car.

When rationing ended in 1954, a cooked breakfast of bacon and eggs was back on the menu.

The 'Go to work on an egg' campaign was launched in 1957, and eggs were suddenly all stamped with the British Lion mark, which showed their grade and packing-station number.

Cereal was very popular with children and was seen as a healthy start to the day. One of the most popular cereals at the time was Kellogg's Frosties, which, of course, are still around today. Many cereals offered free gifts. Corn Flakes featured free submarines, Cowboys and Indians, and military bandsmen. The plastic toy atomic submarines were first given away in 1957 and had even been tested at HMS *Dolphin*, the Royal Navy's submarine base. Corn Flakes had been in short supply during the Second World War. Because of the restrictions on the import of corn, they disappeared from British shelves. Other Kellogg's products during that time could only be bought in the North or in the Midlands.

Children could have jam with their toast, and one of the most popular brands was Robertson's, which gave away free golliwog badges.

By the time the children were having their breakfast, the milkman would have delivered the milk to the house, the postman would have been and the morning paper would have arrived, delivered by a paper boy keen to make extra money. These were all services that people took for granted and that always arrived at near enough the same time during the week. Dad was likely to be a manual or office worker, and if he didn't walk, cycle or catch the bus to work, he would get on one of the many trains, which were much better used and covered a more extensive area.

Once Dad had set off for work, the children would be got ready to leave for school, complete with their satchels, pencils, books and anything else they might need during the day. Undoubtedly, most would walk to school with little fear of car accidents or anything else. Many would end up with scraped knees after running to get to class or the playground on time.

Preschool children stayed at home with their mothers as they did the daily chores. Prams, complete with babies or toddlers, could be seen parked outside grocers' shops while mothers shopped inside with little worry of any harm coming to their children.

A week was set out in days for a housewife. Mondays would be 'wash day', Tuesday would be 'ironing day' and so on throughout the week. Sunday was meant to be a day of rest, although there was still much cooking and washing-up to be done by Mum, including cooking the Sunday roast.

Bread and dripping was popular and would sometimes be given to children for breakfast; it was thought to be a healthy snack at the time. Many children returned home at dinner time for a cooked meal before going back to school. After the rationing of the Second World War, mothers did their best to keep their family well fed on whatever was available.

Some children stayed at school for school dinners, which, at the time, were relatively cheap. Many complained because the food wasn't too good, with meat full of fat and gristle. Children had to clear their plates, and were told off or, in some cases, given the cane if they didn't finish their meal. This went on well into the 1960s. After the hard times of the Second World War, many teachers became very annoyed if they saw any food left. In reality, children were suddenly a lot better fed at home and, in many cases, school dinners to them were quite disgusting.

At home, people had set days for certain meals. Sunday's meal might be roast beef and Yorkshire puddings, with other meals on a set day throughout the week, including fish on a Friday.

Picnics and days out were accompanied by sandwiches with fish paste or spam and bottles of pop.

There were regular visitors to a 1950s household. As well as visits from neighbours and relatives, there were early-morning deliveries from the postman, milkman and paper boy. Then there was the coalman (all homes had coal fires) with his horse and cart, as well as other tradesmen, including the rag-and-bone man and the local chimney sweep.

Things within a 1950s household changed greatly over the decade. At the beginning of the decade, there were few or no electrical appliances, no gadgets to help with housework or other daily chores. Houses would have been sparse, with little decoration or comfort. Utility furniture was very plain, dark and uncomfortable. This all changed as the decade moved on. By the late 1950s, most houses had appliances such as refrigerators, vacuum cleaners, television, radio and record players.

Kenneth Wood began producing kitchen appliances in 1947, including an electric toaster that could toast both sides of the bread without it having to be taken out. By 1950, under the brand name 'Kenwood', he revolutionised post-war kitchens with the launch of the Kenwood Chef at the Ideal Home Exhibition. The labour-saving device was a must-have for lots of housewives and many shops were soon sold out. By 1956, Kenwood was an international success with a £1.5 million turnover. With its 400 staff, the company produced labour-saving products such as liquidisers, hand mixers and steam irons. By the end of the decade, many appliances that were once seen as futuristic and unobtainable were now part of every household. Housewives now had more time to themselves and most houses had electric stoves, toasters and kettles. Some appliances, such as washing machines and refrigerators, were still deemed quite expensive and many households didn't have them until the 1960s.

DIY was almost unheard of, but nailing sheets of hardboard over ornate doors, fireplaces and stairways was seen as very modern. Once the job was completed, neighbours would be invited around to see the handiwork and marvel at how the ornate woodwork was no longer a collector of dust. They would then return to their houses and 'modernise' them in the same way.

With new gadgets and appliances, the kitchen was changed so that everything was close to hand. Formica changed the look of the kitchen. Out went the dreary pre-war appearance and in came fitted kitchens with easy-to-clean Formica worktops.

Over the next decade, the look of the house became much more modern with up-to-date furniture, appliances and technology, such as televisions and compact record players. The house of 1959 was totally different to the one at the beginning of the decade when Britain was still recovering from the Second World War.

More modern music, fashion, entertainment and furnishings led to a vast improvement in the lives of people over the decade, and Britain had changed totally by the time it was approaching the 1960s.

2

Toys and Games

Toys and games have changed greatly over the years. Back in the 1950s, children knew no fear; the world was out there for them to explore. There were no health and safety laws and there were great adventures to be had. The only thing to worry about was being caught by the local bobby while getting up to no good, and being taken home to your parents for a clip 'round the ear! All children played outside in the 1950s. Imagination played a big part in children's lives. The nearby woods were the perfect place for building dens, climbing trees or pretending to be Robin Hood and his Merry Men, Davy Crockett, Roy Rogers or Ivanhoe. Streets would be full of children with scraped knees and scuffed shoes, having the time of their lives. Football would be played on the road with no fear of a car disrupting the fun. Boys would construct their own go-karts out of a plank of wood, four discarded pram wheels and a length of rope tied to the front to aid steering. Some had brakes of simple construction, while others ran uncontrollably downhill, sometimes tipping out their occupants at the bottom of the street. Every dad could construct a go-kart but most boys liked to build their own, mostly out of spare parts found lying around.

Hula hoops were extremely popular, especially with girls, although everyone could be seen using them. The craze spread across the world in the late 1950s and people could be seen hula-hooping in the street, on the beach or at holiday camps. Housewives saw them as a way to stay fit and trim, and children saw them just as a great fun toy that was cheap and cheerful. Arthur Melin and Richard Knerr founded the company Wham-O in California in 1948 and went on to produce the plastic Hula-Hoops that were soon in demand all over the world. They got the idea after seeing Australian children playing with wooden hoops during gym classes. They changed the material to plastic, and the hoops became an overnight success, with 25 million selling in the first two months.

Matchbox cars were first introduced in 1953. They were so named because they came in boxes similar to those containing matches. Matchbox was a brand produced by Lesney, which was founded by Jack Odell, Leslie Smith and Rodney Smith. A model of Queen Elizabeth II's coronation coach became Lesney's first toy to sell more than a million. The first Matchbox product was designed by Jack Odell. Odell's daughter attended a school which would only allow children to bring in toys small enough to fit in a matchbox. Odell scaled down Lesney's red-and-green roadroller, and the toy became the prototype for Matchbox's first 1-75 vehicle. Soon, it was joined by a dumper truck and cement mixer, and the three toys became the beginning of the Matchbox range. Other models were soon added to the range, including cars such as the Ford Zodiac, MG Midget and Vauxhall Cresta. At first, all models were based on British cars, but as the company grew European and American cars were also included. Their reasonable prices meant that most boys in the 1950s had a collection of Matchbox cars.

Dinky Cars were produced by Meccano Ltd, who also made Hornby Railways. Their scaled-down vehicles became very popular with boys in the post-war years.

When Corgi produced their own cars, which, unlike their rivals, included clear plastic windows, Dinky retaliated – in 1956, they produced a series of more sophisticated models, which included suspension and detailed interiors. Tri-ang produced their own range in 1959, which competed with Dinky, Corgi and Matchbox. They included many British vehicles but were slightly more expensive and never sold in the numbers that their rivals did.

Frank Hornby came up with the idea for Meccano back in 1901 and had called it 'Mechanics Made Easy'. The toy consisted of small metal strips with holes, plates, pulleys, gears, and nuts and bolts. The toy was seen as educational as well as fun, but very soon demand started to exceed supply, so Hornby set up a factory in Liverpool to cope with the additional manufacturing needs. The kits became more and more popular and were soon on sale around the world. By 1907, Hornby had registered the name Meccano, and seven years later an additional factory had been opened to keep up with demand. By the 1950s, Meccano was a well-loved toy, but, because of the Second World War, production was interrupted, when the factory at Binns Road in Liverpool was used to help the war effort. The Korean War in 1950 also disrupted production because of metal shortages, but by the mid-1950s production was back to normal. Children loved playing with Meccano in the 1950s, and what they constructed was limited only by their imagination. Cranes were a popular item to construct, as were cars, boats and aeroplanes.

Games in the street, as well as at school, included football, playing conkers, marbles, cricket, hide and seek, and 'it' (also called tag).

Conkers were collected from the nearest horse-chestnut tree, and were much prized by boys. A string would be fed through the conker and the game involved hitting it against an opponent's conker, taking it in turns until one broke and shattered. Every time a conker won, it was given a point and the conker with the highest number was the most desirable. There were various ways to aid winning: one was to soak the conker in vinegar, which would harden it and give it more chance of winning; another way was to keep the conker for a year, which would also make it harder. However, what boy would want to wait a year before he could compete?

All boys had a collection of marbles and these could be added to by playing opponents in the street or playground. A shallow hole would be dug in the mud and players would compete against opponents.

Toy cookers were popular with girls, who wanted to copy their mothers. They smelled of the methylated spirit used within them, but were considered safe for small children to use. How things have changed! Some toy cookers would burn paraffin discs, which were placed beneath the rings. They were then lit, and girls could cook small pieces of meat, etc., with a piece of lard in small frying pans. This would then be served up to Dad, who had to eat it if he wanted to keep his little girl happy. What would health and safety rules make of this today?

Airfix kits were very popular with boys. One of the first commercial plastic kits was sold through Woolworths in 1954. It featured a model of Sir Francis Drake's *Golden Hind*. The retail price was 2 shillings, and the kit was sold in a plastic bag with a paper header to keep the cost down. It was a huge success, and very soon afterwards the first model aircraft was produced, featuring the Supermarine Spitfire, issued in 1955.

Playing cards, completing jigsaws or playing board games were all very popular with children. Educational card games for kids were first brought out in Victorian times, and many still survive today. 'Happy Families', amazingly, was invented back in 1851 and has been enjoyed ever since.

The game involved using a special pack of cards featuring various members of different families, all with different trades. The idea was to match as many as possible. Using an ordinary pack of cards, games such as Snap, Old Maid and Patience could be played. Card games and board games were immensely popular before the advent of television.

Every family had several board games, which would be played on quiet evenings or rainy days. One of the most popular was Monopoly, which was created in 1934, although the idea for it went back much further. It was an incredibly well-liked board game in the 1950s, usually played by four members of the same family or with several friends. The board, counters and houses have become iconic over the years, and are instantly recognisable nowadays. The counters included a Scottie dog, a ship, an iron, a book, a top hat, a racing car and a thimble. The idea was to make your way around the board, collecting £200 when you passed go, and buying property along the way. The winner was the person who ended up with all of the money.

Another popular board game was Cluedo. It was produced by Waddingtons and was first available in 1949. The game featured six characters, including Miss Scarlett, Colonel Mustard, Mrs White, Reverend Green, Mrs Peacock and Professor Plum. The aim of the game was to get around the board, which included several different rooms of a mansion, collecting clues, while trying to deduce who murdered the game's victim, Dr Black. The idea for the game was devised by Anthony E. Pratt, who was a solicitor's clerk from Birmingham.

Snakes and Ladders involved rolling a dice to proceed to the top of the board. If a player landed on a ladder, he could go up it, but if he landed on a snake, he had to go down it. The game originally came from India, where it was known as Moksha Patam, and it eventually made its way to England. Milton Bradley later produced a similar game in America called Chutes and Ladders. Tiddlywinks, Battleships, Dominoes, Noughts and Crosses, Chess, and Draughts were other regularly played games. Battleships involved plotting and sinking an opponent's battleships, which were drawn on graph paper. Dad's spare pools coupons often came in handy for the purpose! A grid would be marked out with letters along one side and numbers along the other side. A player had to guess the position of an opponent's battleship by giving grid references such as 'A24'.

Tiddlywinks featured small coloured plastic discs, which had to be flipped, using another disc, into a pot. It is considered a child's game, but in 1955, the University of Cambridge introduced an adult game using tiddlywinks with more complex rules, strategy and competition. However, no family playing the game in their house in the 1950s would have been concerned by that! It was just a bit of fun.

Scrabble became hugely popular in the 1950s. A variation of the game had been around since the 1930s. The game began to be sold in the UK in 1955 and was manufactured by J. W. Spear's. The game involved spelling out words on a grid using tiles with individual letters on them. Each tile carried its own point score and the winner was the person who had the highest score at the end of the game.

Chess was seen as a game of skill and patience, moving pieces one by one until an opponent was in checkmate. There were undoubtedly many games of chess played in the 1950s, although younger children might have considered it too highbrow and boring. Draughts was a much more fun game for kids!

Bagatelle boards were also extremely popular. You could buy one ready-made from the shop, or, if he was clever, your dad could make you one from old pieces of hardboard and many nails. It was the forerunner to pinball machines, and most boys had one.

Escalado was a horse-racing game that was patented by a Swiss inventor called Arthur Gueydan in 1928. It featured six mechanical horses, and players would try to predict which one was going to win.

Every boy's dream was to own a Hornby train set. Hornby's first train had been released in 1920. It was clockwork O-gauge model. By 1925, electric-powered trains were available but Hornby continued to produce clockwork models until 1937. In 1938, Meccano introduced OO-gauge trains. These were originally known as Hornby Dublo. Production was halted during the Second World War, but resumed in 1948.

After the war, large numbers of tin toys were produced in Japan and exported all over the world. They included robots, spaceships, cars, boats, aeroplanes, animals and other toys. In the late 1950s and 1960s, it was common to see 'Made in Japan' on a variety of cheap items, much in the same way that everything says 'Made in China' today.

Britain produced its own tinplate items. Many young children were lucky to get Tri-ang tin pedal cars for their birthdays or for Christmas.

George and Joseph Lines made wooden toys in the Victorian age, and Lines Brothers Ltd was formed by three of their sons. They commenced selling under the name Tri-ang Railways in 1951. Tri-ang also made other toys, including pressed-steel lorries, buses, delivery vans, cranes and circus lorries, etc.

Boys loved chemistry sets, and they were popular presents for birthdays and Christmas. Amazingly, they contained ingredients such as uranium dust and sodium cyanide. They contained a range of other dangerous chemicals, a microscope, slides, dead butterflies and tweezers etc. Many kits showed you how to make explosive mixtures and how to produce puffs of smoke as seen in magic shows. They were potentially very dangerous but no one ever seemed to come to any harm. By the 1970s, the sets were losing their popularity, and soon after, health and safety rules brought an end to them altogether. They are still looked upon fondly, though, by people reminiscing about their childhood.

Toys of the 1950s were simpler and often involved playing with friends or family members.

Making your own toys could also be a lot of fun. Using two tins, attaching a long piece of string between them and keeping it taut was meant to be a way of making your own telephone, although people were probably more likely to be heard shouting into the tin a short distance away than using the makeshift contraption. If that didn't work, then the cans and string could be used to make stilts. Many kids clunked around like Frankenstein using no more than two old Ovaltine tins fixed to two sets of looped string!

Yo-yos were enjoyed by many in the 1950s, as they had been for decades. They first became popular in Great Britain in the 1920s, although they are much older and originated in Ancient Greece. Many kids of the 1950s learned how to do elaborate tricks with them, the most common being 'Walking the Dog', where the yo-yo would roll across the floor before springing back into its owner's hand.

Making your own model aircraft out of balsa wood was also very popular. Some just glided, but many had built-in engines with small propellers. The problem was that there was no remote control, and you never knew where your plane was going to end up or if it was going to crash into a tree or other obstacle. Most planes flew a few hundred yards and then hit the ground so hard that they shattered. KeilKraft advertised in many magazines of interest to boys, and for 21*s* 7*d* you could buy a ready-made plane complete with 'crash-proof wings'.

Every boy wanted a bicycle and every girl wanted roller skates. Many bikes were either second-hand or built from a collection of bits from old bikes. Dads would paint up second-hand bikes for their kids and no one cared that they weren't new. A dad could also come in very handy when it came to repairing punctures or replacing tyres or chains.

Many adverts appeared in boys' magazines on how to make your own radio (or crystal set). One shilling bought you all the plans and instructions you needed. These were still being advertised in the 1970s, although, by then, it was probably easier to just buy your own radio!

Most children, especially boys, had a hobby. Many collected stamps, which were saved for them by relatives and friends of their parents. Anyone who had a relative who worked abroad or was in the Navy would probably have an excellent collection of foreign and exotic stamps, which would be the envy of friends. Some would be swapped in the playground. Many magazines had stamp clubs and a mixture of foreign stamps could be bought for a shilling.

Although film was relatively expensive, most families had their own camera. One of the cheapest and most popular was the Kodak Brownie 127, which was so simple to operate that a child could use it. Many of the photographs that people treasure of the 1950s were taken by kids, who would sometimes take their camera with them when they ventured out. Many children's first camera, probably given to them for Christmas or birthdays, was a Bakelite Kodak 127. Photographs still weren't taken in the quantities they are today, though, because the film was so dear to get developed.

Other popular hobbies of the time included collecting birds' eggs, writing down car number plates or spotting other items around. Collecting tea cards or cards featuring footballers was also a popular pastime. Children loved collecting things, whether it was stamps, coins or obscure things like keys. The toys and games of the 1950s were, in many cases, geared towards pursuits that involved your friends or other members of your family, and there was certainly a lot of fun to be had by getting other people to join in.

Many games that kept kids happy and content for hours in the 1950s seem quite basic by today's standards, and they're a far cry from the modern computer games played by the new generation of children.

3

School

To children today, the schools of the 1950s would perhaps seem very grim places. Stricter teachers, more punishments, more respect and certainly no talking in class or calling teachers by their first names! However, many children of the 1950s were happy with their lot and remember their school days fondly.

Most children made their own way to school without their parents. Some even walked a couple of miles to get there. Boys would wear grey flannel shorts and long grey socks as part of their uniform. Girls always wore dresses. School caps and berets would also have to be worn if they were part of the uniform, and there would be trouble if a kid was seen without his or hers.

In the winter, small children would be led to school, complete with galoshes (Wellington boots), duffle coats, knitted bobble hats and mittens, while they kicked through dead leaves until they reached the school gates.

School would start at 9 a.m. sharp, and anyone who was late would be in trouble. A bell would be rung to get everybody from the playground into the classroom.

The Butler Education Act of 1944 compelled pupils to say prayers in the morning before they began their lessons. The Act also made sure that every child had ⅓ of a pint of milk a day.

The day would usually start with the morning assembly, which would involve prayers and a talk from the headmaster about school events, bad behaviour or any other matters he wished to discuss. Some schools had 'houses', which children were expected to sit in. The children would then be dismissed from assembly, and would return to their classes, where the register would be called. Children in the 1950s had 'normal' names, like David, Robert, Stephen, Alan or Susan. There were certainly no 'Keanus' or 'DJs' like there are today! Children who had been missing the day before, who hadn't been marked in the register, would have to explain their absence and produce a suitable note from a parent. Truancy would not be tolerated, and, with the teacher knowing the name of every pupil in their class, absent pupils would always be missed. Many of the teachers had served in the Second World War (some in the First World War), and some classrooms seemed to be run in a strict military style. Pupils would normally be called by their surnames, both when the register was called and in the classroom, and pupils would have to reply with 'Yes, sir!' or 'Yes, miss!' Heaven help any pupil who said 'yeah' instead of 'yes'.

Children learned to read from basic *Janet and John* books, and had to write with ink pens that were dipped into inkwells. Many kids would end up with it on their hands, or, worse still, it would blob on their work and there would be trouble with the teacher. All children sat at wooden desks, in rows facing towards the blackboard. When a teacher spoke, they were expected to listen, with no backchat or interruption. Woe betide any child who talked in class!

Teachers could be strict, and boys would get the cane if there were any misdemeanours; girls would be rapped on the knuckles or across the palm of the hand if there was any misbehaving or talking.

Multiplication tables had to be learned and repeated out loud in class. A teacher would test his pupils weekly to see that they knew their tables by firing mathematical questions, much to the panic of many pupils. Strict teachers would shout if the answer was wrong or, perhaps, give the cane or lines.

Subjects included maths, history, geography and physical training (known just as 'PT'). Geography taught children about the capitals of the world, and a map on the wall would show the areas once controlled by the British Empire. Historical lessons covered the reigns of previous monarchs of England.

PT came from a strict teacher, often an ex-Army man, in a games hall complete with a vaulting horse, ropes and a medicine ball. A medicine ball thrown at a boy at speed would probably knock him off his feet. It was meant to be character-building, but probably put many small boys off sport for life. Other sports at school included football, cricket and the dreaded cross-country run. The PT teacher would shout at boys to run faster, but no one would ever see a teacher complete a course! Kids would be taught to swim at the local swimming baths. It was unheard of for a school to have its own swimming pool. Some schools would issue swimming certificates, which would be awarded in assembly, if the pupil managed to swim a certain distance.

Many classrooms had stoves to keep them warm. In the morning, all children would get a bottle of milk to drink, which was ⅓ of a pint. This was seen as a way to keep children healthy, as some might not be getting a very good breakfast at home. Some families were very poor, and undoubtedly some went without a morning snack. Often, in the winter, the milk would be frozen, so it would be left near the stove to thaw out. Many kids wanted to be class monitors and would put their hands up to be chosen. There would be milk monitors, pencil monitors and also monitors for when other items were given out.

Breaks or playtime were keenly looked forward to, and many kids would eagerly watch the clock. There was usually a break in the morning and in the afternoon, with a longer break in the middle of the day for dinner. Children would pour into the playground at these times eager to play conkers or marbles, or to get a gang together to play football, war games or Cowboys and Indians. Inevitably, a fight would break out and everyone would crowd around and encourage one side or another. Eventually a teacher would turn up, break up the fight, give the boys a clip around the ear and send them straight to the headmaster's office. Even if you hadn't started the fight you still got in trouble!

Other games played on the concrete schoolyard would include hide-and-seek (if there was anywhere to hide), tag (also known as 'it') and British Bulldog. Girls would have a long skipping rope and would chant as other girls skipped in and out. Hopscotch would also be played, with a grid marked out on the floor in chalk. Some schools would keep the boys and girls in separate playgrounds and they weren't allow to stray into the other one. If a boy was caught in the girls' playground, he would almost certainly have to see the headmaster and maybe get the cane.

School dinners were subsidised by the government and cost parents about half a crown for the week's meals. This was to make sure that all children had at least one healthy meal a day, as many families were poor and children may have not had all the nutrition they needed. School meals weren't popular with most, and consisted of meat and vegetables with a pudding for afters; examples included jam roly-poly and spotted dick and custard. The meat used for school dinners was like no meat you ever got anywhere else and was quite often very gristly. It must have been bought in cheaply, as with many of the vegetables, which weren't always as good as they should have been. Even so, school dinner ladies made the best of what they had. Some kids even had seconds if any were going. The wartime mentality of eating everything on your plate still continued (even in the 1970s), and children worried about leaving any food uneaten in case it was spotted by a strict teacher and the pupil was given the cane. All in all, school dinners probably aren't remembered too fondly!

In class, children had to be well-behaved, stay very quiet and not talk among each other. Discipline could be strict and there would certainly be no talking back to the teacher.

It wasn't unusual, if children were chatting, for the teacher to throw a piece of chalk or blackboard eraser at the talking pupil. If it hit him then that was just bad luck and there would certainly be no complaints of assault from either parents or the police. The teacher was always right (even when he was wrong!). Punishments in class included a slap on the legs, a sharp jerk on your ear, being made to keep your hands on your head or having to stand in the corner. More serious crimes (which really amounted to nothing) would result in the cane or the strap. Some kids would be sent out in the corridor to face the wall, and would dread that the headmaster might pass and ask why they were there. Other children would be sent straight to see the headmaster, and panic would set in as they waited outside his office knowing full well that they would probably get the cane.

However, there were also fun things to do at school, like drawing and painting, using plasticine, and making papier-mâché items, like decorated plates and saucers. The excitement came when you took the item home to show your mum!

Religion played a big part in school life. As mentioned earlier, prayers were said at the beginning of the day and also sometimes at the end. Hymns would be sung, with words read from a large song sheet. Many pupils enjoyed singing even if they weren't religious at all. Bible stories were constantly read but stories like Joseph and his coat of many colours were, especially to young children, seen as just as exciting as tales of the Arabian Nights. School holidays revolved around religion, with the main ones being Easter and Christmas. The lead up to both events seemed exciting, with lots of stories. Christmas was probably the best, with tales of the Three Wise Men and the birth of Jesus. When combined with making decorations for the Christmas tree and the home, it must have been one of the most anticipated times at school.

At the age of eleven, children would take the eleven-plus exam. Passing ensured that they went to the local grammar school. Failing meant that you went to the secondary modern, where your prospects were seen to be worse. The eleven-plus exam was created as part of the Butler Education Act of 1944. It included arithmetic, writing and general problem-solving – testing general knowledge and applying logic to solve simple problems. This was ideal for boys, who regularly pretended to be spies, creating codes and writing letters in invisible ink. A child's mind in the 1950s was inquisitive and inventive; they enjoyed creating crystal radio sets, making phones from two cans and a piece of string, using chemistry sets, and playing Battleships and war games. Perhaps a boy's mind in the 1950s was more suited to an exam like the eleven-plus.

The exam was taken in the last year of junior school and was meant to show which way a child would develop in later life – if they would be suited to academic, technical or functional work. The results of the test were meant to match the pupil with the school that would best help them with their future careers. However, technical schools never materialised as envisaged, and the results of the eleven-plus just pointed to a child either passing or failing.

At the end of the term, the teacher would make up a school report that would be taken home and shown to the pupil's parents. Many were harsh and fault-finding, and many children worried about taking them home. A slip had to be signed by one of the parents to say that they'd seen it. Having a good report was something to be proud of, although probably most reports included the phrase 'could do better'!

Waiting in class to see who had or had not passed the eleven-plus was also a daunting experience – exciting for the ones who had passed, but a long walk home to tell their parents for those who hadn't!

Some children also attended Sunday school, which was run by the church and featured all things religious, but also had fetes, events, picnics and other outings.

Once at secondary school or grammar school, a lot of the fun of primary school seemed to disappear. There were more subjects to learn and certainly more homework. Languages were taught, although the average child in the 1950s had little chance of meeting someone who was French, German or Spanish, and, at the time, no one travelled abroad much. Perhaps teachers expected another war around the corner and felt a foreign language would come in handy! Other additional subjects would include woodwork for boys and domestic science (cookery) for girls. These subjects were seen to help pupils when they left school. For the same reason, girls would also take typing and needlework. However, never the twain would mix; girls certainly weren't allowed to do woodwork and boys could never decide that they wanted to take domestic science or typing. There were set subjects for boys and set subjects for girls, and, at the time, no one would dare suggest differently.

There was a wider variety of sports played at secondary school, including football, cricket, tennis, rugby, rounders, running, javelin, shot-putting and other 'sports day' type activities. The chances were that if you didn't like your PT teacher at junior school, you were going to like the one at secondary school even less. On the whole, most PT teachers were bully-boy types, and this sort of mentality carried on for decades to come.

There were petty rules about uniform. A boy could get told off, or worse, for not having his tie done up properly or for not wearing a cap or other essential part of the outfit. A teacher could explode if he saw a boy with his hands anywhere but by his sides, with cries of 'Get your hands out of your pockets, boy'! In many ways, a lot of the teachers had the mentality of their army days and, although schools were meant to have moved on since Victorian times, discipline still played a large part of school life.

Secondary school tried to teach you all you needed to know for when you left school, although most subjects, such as chemistry and physics, played little part in pupils' later lives. Much to the dismay of school children in the 1950s, the school leaving age had been raised to fifteen years old in 1948. It wasn't until 1972 that the leaving age was raised again to sixteen.

Altogether, schools of the 1950s were a lot stricter than they are today, although children still found lots to enjoy. Perhaps most, though, looked forward to the day when their school days would be over for good!

4

Outdoor Activities

Every bomb site became a battleground for boys playing
war games, and every wood became a haven for building
dens or pretending to be Robin Hood and his Merry Men.
The streets were playgrounds, with games of football,
hopscotch, skipping, cricket and general larking around
taking place. With few cars or other vehicles passing, it
meant that the streets were a safe place to play. There was
a lot to fire a child's imagination, including adventure series
on the television, the latest blockbuster at the local cinema
or an adventure serial on the radio. Imagination meant that
you could be anything you wanted, including a cowboy, a
soldier, a knight, an outlaw or even a spaceman. There were
many mock battles fought. Children, especially boys, who
wanted to play war games would chant, with their arms
around each other's shoulders, 'who wants a game of war'
or 'we won the war in 1944' until enough boys had gathered
to play a game. The same process continued into the 1970s.
Once enough boys had been found, two people would pick
sides, choosing people from the line-up. It wasn't much fun
if you were the last boy chosen. Some kids would even have
their own toy guns, complete with caps, to shoot each other.
Some just used their fingers to replicate guns and made a
firing noise when shooting. Many players who had been
'shot' got up again and again to continue playing, and the

whole game went on until their mums, one by one, called them in for tea or to go to bed.

Old bomb sites could sometimes be a dangerous place to play, and occasionally an unexploded bomb would be found and the area would be cordoned off until the bomb was dealt with. However, not all explosives were reported, and it wasn't too unusual to hear of a kid who had found a Mills bomb (or hand grenade) and taken it home to keep as a souvenir in their wardrobe. Amazingly, it was unheard of for one to explode, and many of the dangers posed weren't obvious to a boy keeping one in his wardrobe or under the bed. Even guns were found and taken home.

Choosing someone to be 'it' involved picking someone by chanting

Eeny, meeny, miny, moe,
Catch a tiger by the toe.
If he hollers, let him go,
Eeny, meeny, miny, moe.

and slowly counting along the group. The poem also featured various other words instead of 'tiger'.

Another way of picking someone was by using the chant 'one potato, two potato, three potato four, five potato, six potato, seven potato, more'.

There were also games involving many participants, including 'ring a ring o' roses' and 'what's the time, Mr Wolf?'

Children playing 'ring a ring o' roses' would gather in a circle and chant,

Ring a ring of roses.
A pocketful of posies,
Atishoo, Atishoo,
We all fall down!

The game has been played around the world for hundreds of years, and many people link it to the plague, although this connection only appeared in the 1950s.

'What's the time, Mr Wolf?' involved one player playing the part of Mr Wolf. Mr Wolf would stand opposite the other players, facing away from them. The players would then chant 'what's the time, Mr Wolf?' and Mr Wolf would reply with a time. If it was '3 o'clock', the players would take three steps closer. In response to the chant, Mr Wolf could also answer 'dinner time', which would then allow him to try and catch one of the players, so that they became the new 'Mr Wolf'.

Cherry knocking (also sometimes called 'knock down ginger') consisted of someone daring another kid to knock on a door before running off. There would be much laughing when someone came to the door to find no one there! There was always the worry of someone fetching a policeman, and the offending kid would get a clip around the ear or, worse still, would be taken home to their parents, where Dad would give them another clip around the ear and a good telling off. Children would also tie string to a few door knockers at the same time so that they could knock on several doors from a safe distance.

If there was a nearby park, kids would play on the swings, roundabouts, see-saws, witch's hat, maypole and slide until they were called in for their tea.

As mentioned before, bomb sites made very popular playgrounds and, when they weren't pretending to be cowboys or war heroes, boys would be building dens out of anything they could find. Any spare piece of land or woods would be ideal for making a den. The woods were a much better place to play in, because there were trees to climb and adults couldn't see what they were up to. Many kids would make their own bows and arrows out of twigs and a bit of string, and would pretend to be Robin Hood or

William Tell. *Ivanhoe*, with Roger Moore, was very popular on the television at the time and children would re-enact his adventures. A fallen twig soon became a machine gun for a boy, and he would quickly be machine-gunning his friends with a loud rat-a-tat-tat noise. They would soon all follow suit or pretend to be shot and roll into ditches. Their clothes would be filthy, and so would the kid wearing them, but every mother expected it.

Some boys had real guns, which were used for target practice and other less salubrious activities. Air pistols, at the time, were perfectly legal and it was very rare that anyone got accidently injured.

Fishing was also very popular with boys. If there was a river, stream or, better still, the sea nearby, many boys would make it their aim to catch some fish to take home for tea. If a proper fishing rod couldn't be found, makeshift ones could be made. Many kids would make their own fishing poles and lines. Amazingly, nearly every boy had his own pocketknife (or penknife) and no one thought anything of it. It was handy for a variety of uses, including cutting snagged fishing line. In reality, many of the fish caught were inedible, and were probably fed to the local cat, but the thrill of going out fishing, and the fun of being out with your mates trying to catch a 'whopper', more than made up for the fact that little was caught.

The coronation of 1953 led to a lot of outdoor activity and celebration. Street parties were held, with plenty of food, games and music. Flags were displayed everywhere, and for children there were competitions like the egg-and-spoon race, the three-legged race and the sack race. Everyone was incredibly patriotic and most streets had their own party, with plenty of fun and food for the kids.

Many magazines advertised projects for adventurous boys. One, in the *Boy's Own* magazine of 1954, offered plans telling you how to construct your own canoe. The instructions, from Tyne Folding Boats Ltd, cost 1s 6d, although building the actual boat proved a lot more costly!

The *Boy's Own* magazine of April 1954 also promoted 'a sport rapidly gaining popularity in Britain', called korfball. Although played at competition level nowadays, most people would struggle to think what it is. The two-page advert stated that it was the game of the future and combined handball and basketball. It had originated in Holland and is still more popular there than it is in England.

The magazine also promoted yachting for boys, but this was probably out of reach for many families and only a select few would have taken part.

Games of football could be seen in every street and kids would gather together after school and pick sides or just have a general kick around, with coats or jumpers used to mark goal posts. If a football wasn't available, an old can would be used instead.

Boys loved joining the Cubs or the Scouts and would often go in groups on camping trips. Equally, girls joined the Brownies or the Guides. A Scout leader would teach boys things like orienteering, bird spotting, how to start a fire and a whole range of other activities. The regular camping trips would include singing songs around a camp fire. All would-be Scouts would have to learn their 'allegiance to the queen' speech and have a uniform complete with shorts, shirt, scarf and woggle. It all seemed very adventurous for a boy back then, and sleeping under the stars and taking part in varied activities during the day seemed very exciting. Badges could be earned for different tasks and would be sewn to the sleeves of the Scout's shirt.

Parents also took their children on camping trips. By the 1950s, camping had become a bit more modern, with sleeping bags, touring stoves for hot meals and even mosquito nets (although no mosquitoes were to be found in Britain!). In the later 1950s, some of the people who had cars were also fortunate enough to have caravans, and would take their family to the seaside or countryside for short holidays.

School holidays were eagerly awaited. The long hot weeks of summer led to much fun and mischief, including building dens, climbing trees, exploring building sites and bombed land and generally having a good time.

New building sites offered a wealth of opportunity to play or have an adventure. Running along walls and jumping off the end like a commando or superhero, playing hide-and-seek, running through drains, mixing up cement, pinching materials for dens or knocking glass bottles off walls could take all day. Usually the adventure ended when someone complained or the local bobby came along. Building sites weren't cordoned off like they are today, and children, especially boys, would see the area as an adventure playground.

Spring brought new flowers and new wildlife, including many new birds. Children also enjoyed bird spotting as well as collecting eggs from nests. The rule was to only take one egg from each nest. Once they'd scaled the tree and collected the egg, they would take it home, prick it at each end with a needle and carefully blow out the contents. Every boy had a collection of bird's eggs and knew which one belonged to which bird. Of course, the practice is totally illegal nowadays. Boys would also have butterfly nets, and would catch as many butterflies as they could and pin the different varieties to a board. It all seems cruel nowadays, although the poor insects would be dead long before they were pinned. In the 1950s, the fields, gardens and meadowlands offered an abundance of birds and insects, with a huge variety of butterflies. Unfortunately, they're not seen in such great numbers today. Ladybirds were once seen in their thousands, whereas today it's rare to spot even one.

Searching for snakes and slow-worms was another enjoyed pastime, and many children would show off any slow-worms they found to their mates, most of whom were too scared to touch them. Every boy took a jam jar to the local pond or stream to collect tadpoles, and marvelled as they slowly turned into frogs on the window ledge. Most were then released again, as it seemed impossible to feed them. Finding a full-size frog was a treasure. If you knew how to keep and look after it, you'd be the envy of your friends. The same net that had been used for catching butterflies could also be used for catching tadpoles.

The summer holidays seemed to go on forever, and with an inquisitive mind every day seemed to be an adventure. It was a sad time when the holidays were over and everybody had to return to school, but there were still the evenings and weekends to have fun.

Autumn was a good time to search for horse chestnuts, better known to schoolkids everywhere as conkers. The conker season fell between September and October. Finding a suitable horse-chestnut tree was just the start. Collecting as many conkers as you could was in itself seen as an achievement and could make you the envy of your friends. The playground was soon busy with children, mainly boys, with their prized conkers on a piece of string.

Once the winter set in, there was still much to do outside. One of the best times was Guy Fawkes Night, or Bonfire Night, on 5 November. As much wood as possible, along with anything else that would burn, would be collected together on wasteland to make a huge bonfire. Kids boasted about whose area had the biggest bonfire. The lead-up to bonfire night would involve children making a Guy out of old clothes, which they would then travel around the streets with, asking people 'Penny for the Guy?' Most people would give the kids a penny or, if they were lucky, a shilling; it might even be a florin if they were very lucky. Undoubtedly, most of the money made would be spent on fireworks, which were only on sale around Guy Fawkes Night. Anyone could buy them and there were no age restrictions as to who could purchase them. A lot of mischief could be had with bangers, but the local bobby often made sure that the culprits were caught and taken back to their parents.

Bangers cost 1*d* and other fireworks were dearer. These included Roman candles, rockets and Catherine wheels. Most families had a small firework display in the back garden or yard, and Dad would always be given the responsible job of lighting them. Rockets were usually placed in a milk bottle, and then the blue touchpaper was lit and everyone stood well back. The fireworks were nothing like they are today but, even so, seemed amazing at the time.

The approach to Guy Fawkes Night included Halloween on 31 October. Some mothers would hollow out and carve faces in turnips, and place a candle inside so that their kids could go out collecting a 'penny for the Guy'. The event was never as popular here as it was in America, but for British children, it was seen as more of a lead-up to the main event of Bonfire Night.

Everyone came out on Bonfire Night and the fire was lit by a responsible adult. Unless some unruly kids had got to it first and set fire to it early! The fire would give out tremendous heat, so children were supervised by their parents. The Guy, which had previously made them all so much money, ended up on the fire. It was easy to make a new one for the following year's celebrations. Some people would bake potatoes in the embers of the fire, as well as cooking Spanish chestnuts, which could be collected during the lead-up to the event. Small children were happy with sparklers, waving them about and making patterns. When everyone went home and was in bed, the flames of the fire could still be seen when they closed their eyes, and everything smelled of smoke for days after.

Christmas holidays were shorter and colder than the summer holidays, but the anticipation of Christmas Day made it seem like no other time of the year. Once Christmas morning was over, it would be straight out to see your pals to show off your new bikes, roller skates, toys or games.

The year seemed to have a more set pattern in the 1950s. Hot in the summer, cold in the winter. If you lived in the North, you would no doubt have a sledge, probably built by your dad for when the heavy snowfall came, or perhaps skates for when the local duck pond froze over.

All children played out in the 1950s, so if one was indoors, it was probably because they were ill, naughty or doing chores for their mothers. In some ways, there was never a more exciting time to be a boy.

5

Childhood Illnesses

Childhood brought with it a collection of illnesses, including mumps, measles and influenza. If one child came down with any infectious illness then it was pretty certain that everyone in their class at school would also get it.

Polio was a killer, and most classes had at least one child who had leg irons because of it. The disease struck fear into the hearts of parents. There were over 45,000 cases during the 1950s, and hundreds of people died from the illness. Contracting polio meant that a child could be disabled for life. Some survivors of the disease were unable to breathe unaided, so had to spend their days in an iron lung. Other, previously healthy, children were paralysed in one or more of their limbs. The disease was much feared and could close schools, cinemas and any other place of entertainment.

Two vaccines for polio were developed in the 1950s. The first was developed by Jonas Salk by injecting a dose of killed poliovirus. It was tested in 1952 and announced to the world in 1955. It reduced the number of cases of polio drastically. Albert Sabin went on to develop an oral polio vaccine, which was licensed in 1962. This type of polio vaccine was given with a lump of sugar.

Measles affected most children and started with a fever, cough, runny nose and red eyes. Shortly after, a rash would appear. In classrooms, it was highly contagious. In the 1950s, measles could still be a killer, and hundreds of people died in Britain because of it. The worst epidemic in recent years had been in 1941, when 1,145 died as a result of contracting the illness. Measles could also lead to breathing, eyesight and neurological problems. Later, measles vaccines reduced the amount of reported cases greatly.

The vaccine was developed by Maurice Ralph Hilleman, who also produced vaccines for mumps, hepatitis A, hepatitis B, chickenpox, meningitis, pneumonia and *Haemophilus influenzae*. In doing so, he saved millions of lives.

German measles (rubella) caused a rash, fever and swollen glands, and was again highly contagious and so easily caught in a 1950s classroom, which usually contained more than thirty children.

Mumps was another inevitable illness during childhood. It caused swelling to the face as well as fever and headaches. In children, it generally ran its course over several weeks without any major complications.

Chickenpox was another highly contagious disease, spread by coughing and sneezing, and produced a rash, fever, headaches and aching muscles.

Meningitis could be fatal and was another airborne infection. In 1944, it was discovered that penicillin had some effect against the disease.

The illnesses mentioned were all pretty serious, and most children contracted some, if not all, of them. Many children enjoyed being off school and taking it easy in bed while they read comics and their mothers fussed around them.

Doctors were always happy to visit their patients in the 1950s, and if a child was sick and bedridden, they wouldn't have to be dragged to the surgery. This contained the illness and stopped it from infecting other people. The doctor would visit on the same day when he was on his rounds. Of course, that's all changed nowadays! With the worry of infections such as polio, a child was best isolated, not only from his or her classmates but also from other children in the waiting room of the doctor's surgery. In the 1950s, doctors' surgeries were nothing like they are today. They'd usually be in a converted house, which consisted of a waiting room and a few other rooms with, at the most, three doctors. Most people always saw the same doctor. Some could be quite aloof and out of touch with the people they dealt with. However, most people had a good relationship with their doctor, who may well have been present at the birth of the patient visiting him.

Coughs, colds and flu seemed to be a lot worse when you were a child, and would often start with a very chesty cough. All mothers had their own remedies, and one was rubbing goose fat on the child's chest to relieve congestion. Sore throats were also meant to be cured with a teaspoon of goose grease. Vicks VapoRub was also rubbed on the chest to relieve congestion and sinus problems. Cough syrups and sweets were used to ease the pain of a sore throat.

Virol malt extract was given to children as well as castor oil, cod liver oil and syrup of figs. Olive oil was also given for coughs, as well as being rubbed on sore chests. A sock or wet bandage could also be placed on the throat, if it was sore, as a home cure.

Scraped knees were treated with iodine, which stung and also stained your knees yellow. Every mum had a bottle kept in the kitchen, as accidents with over-adventurous kids seemed to happen often. Elastoplasts were regularly used for grazed heads, cut knees and hands. After a visit to your mum, a few tears and a cuddle, together with some iodine and an Elastoplast, it was soon time to return outside for more adventures.

The founding of the NHS in 1948 meant free health treatment for all, and undoubtedly saved the lives of thousands of children as a consequence.

The thought of the school dentist was enough to put fear into any school child. The dentist seemed relentless in his pursuit of either filling or pulling teeth. Many were drilled, all without anaesthetic, with slow-speed drills that were not only painful but also slow going. The dentist was also overkeen to remove teeth, which at the time was seen as a cure-all. Gas was given through a rubber mask placed over the face. The gas seemed to give you strange dreams even after it had worn off. Nowadays, none of the teeth removed back then would be removed today, and teeth are certainly filled a lot less. Anyone who lived through the 1950s is probably either toothless or has a mouth full of silver-coloured fillings.

Tonsillitis, which was a contagious condition, often meant a visit to the doctor and a trip to the hospital to have them removed. Many cases of tonsillitis would have settled down by themselves, but in the 1950s it was common practice to remove them. Every year, around 200,000 operations were performed. Many children returned to school boasting of the ice cream they were given after the operation.

The nit nurse was a regular visitor to schools, and she would check for head lice, which, at the time, were quite common and would easily spread throughout a class. Fine metal combs would be taken through the child's hair, desperately trying to find the dreaded head lice. Once they were found, the child was sent home and wasn't allowed back until the head lice were completely gone. The nit nurse seemed to gain pleasure in humiliating children, and the implication was that the child was somehow unclean. Many would have their hair cut short by their parents, and a greasy product would be applied to the hair. It also gave off a strange smell, which was sure to let everyone know that you'd had an infestation. It all added to the embarrassment.

Children also had their eyesight checked, as well as hearing tests. A school optician would produce a large eye chart and would get the pupil to read letters from each line. Depending on how far down the chart he could read, an assessment was made of his eyesight. Colour-blindness tests were also performed, with a child having to spy numbers in an array of different coloured spots. Many children wore National Health glasses and some, who suffered from a lazy eye, would have an Elastoplast stuck over one lens. If you wore glasses, names like 'four eyes', 'speccy' or 'swot' weren't uncommon. Many children hated to wear glasses, especially when most of their friends didn't have to wear them. The fear of bullying meant that many would take them off when they got to the school gates, although they would have needed to put them back on to see the blackboard!

Many childhood illnesses were still killers in the 1950s. Apart from polio, there was also whooping cough, appendicitis and flu. Boys would return to school after having their appendixes out and proudly show off the scar.

As mentioned earlier, childhood illnesses meant the child was sent straight to bed and the doctor would come around and visit. There was no hanging around in waiting rooms for contagious children; polio was as feared as cancer back then.

The rhyme 'coughs and sneezes spread diseases' was known by every schoolchild. Everyone carried a handkerchief in those days and was encouraged to cover their mouth and nose with it if they were about to sneeze or cough. A single sneeze could eventually infect a classroom, so it was very important to try and stop germs spreading.

All children hated the visit by the school doctor, who always wanted them to drop their pants and cough. It was a strange practice that went on for many years, and most people still don't know the reason for it!

The BCG (standing for Bacillus Calmette–Guérin) injection was feared by most children. Most kids had never had an injection before, and this one was more painful than most. In 1953, Great Britain introduced a universal immunisation programme and the injection was given to all schoolchildren at the age of thirteen years old. It was also given to people in high-risk groups. It protected against tuberculosis. The programme was effective in eliminating TB in Britain, with cases only reappearing here in recent years. Some kids would boast that 'they didn't feel a thing' while others would tell tall tales of the needle going in one side of the arm and coming out of the other! Everyone who had it had a sore arm for days and would have to sleep on their other side at night.

Popular remedies and medicines of the day included syrup of figs (for constipation), Beecham's Pills and Bile Beans (both laxatives), Vapex inhalers (for colds), Lucozade (to build up children's vitality) and Scott's Emulsion, which was a variety of cod liver oil, calcium and sodium and was advertised as 'as palatable as milk'. Try telling that to the kids who had to take it! Rosehip syrup contained vitamin C and was used to keep colds at bay. Also available were Potter's Catarrh pastilles, which were for coughs, colds and hay fever.

Mothers had their own home-made recipes, such as a mixture of sugar, lemon and butter for sore throats. Cod liver oil was given liberally and most kids hated it.

With so many kids playing outdoors, accidents were commonplace and, especially after the summer holidays, it wasn't uncommon to have at least one boy in class with a broken arm set in plaster. Common accidents involved falling off bikes, falling out of trees or falling off walls. Everything was seen as an adventure, and many boys somehow managed to split their heads open and would end up at the X-ray department of the local hospital. It was all part of growing up back then. Even the local playground could be a source of accidents, and many children were hurt by swings or see-saws. The concrete floors of playgrounds made the damage even worse, especially when you fell over or came off something.

Headaches always seemed worse when you were a kid. Treatment included Alka-Seltzer tablets, which were dissolved in water. Their slogan was 'there's nothing like Alka-Seltzer for headaches and indigestion'.

A broken arm was almost a badge of honour, and everyone in class after the summer holidays would be examining the arm set in plaster and would maybe write their name on it. The itch of an arm in plaster would be unbearable, and all sorts of instruments, including rulers and knitting needles, would be used to try and scratch it. It would be a great relief when it finally came off six weeks later.

Once you'd had all the major illnesses, such as measles and mumps, you built up an immunity to them and, if you were lucky, never got them again. Many illnesses never quite seemed as bad as they did when you first had them in childhood.

6

Sweets and Chocolate

With the vast array of chocolates and sweets around nowadays, it's hard to imagine a time when there was a shortage.

Sweets and chocolate were still rationed at the beginning of the 1950s and coupons had to be used from a ration book to buy them. Popular sweets of the day included dolly mixture, raspberry drops, Pontefract cakes, gobstoppers, sherbet lemons, Fruit Salads, Black Jacks and toffees. All were kept in glass jars behind the counter. Most children would only have a penny or two to spend, but a penny would buy four of each sweet. There were also Mars bars, which were considered a real treat at $5d$. Sweet cigarettes were popular, with boys copying their favourite film stars and pretending to smoke on the way home from the shop. There were also Rowntree's fruit gums, Barratt's sherbet fountains, Spangles at $3d$ a packet and boxes of chocolates such as Clarnico Regency Candies.

Sweet rationing came to an end in 1953. Some shops gave away free sweets to mark the occasion. The biggest seller, when rationing ended, was toffee apples. Also much in demand were nougat and liquorice strips. A firm in Clapham marked the day by giving 800 children free lollipops during their midday break. A London sweet factory opened its doors on the day and handed out free sweets to anyone who wanted them. Adults also took advantage of the end of rationing and queued up for boiled sweets and boxes of chocolates for their wives. There was no shortage of supply of sweets, unlike when the government first tried the idea of ending sweet rationing in 1949. At that time, demand far outstripped supply and rationing had to be put into place again just four months later. However, sugar was still rationed, so manufacturers had to meet the demand, but with only 54 per cent of the sugar supplies that they once had. The Cocoa, Chocolate & Confectionery Alliance announced that they were very happy with the situation and were sure that they could make it work. Although popular brands soon sold out, there was no panic buying. The reason for this might have been that confectionery prices had doubled over the war years. Rationing had first come into place in January 1940, and rationing of sweets and chocolate began in 1942. With the pressure from sweet and chocolate manufacturers, sugar rationing also came to an end in 1953. Amazingly, spending on sweets and chocolate rose in the first year by £100 million, taking the overall total to £250 million, which was described by the confectionery industry as a boom as 'dynamic as any in the industry's history'.

A visit to the sweet shop was a treat for any kid. Whether with an odd penny or their pocket money, it was almost something mystical. Sweets would be weighed out as 2 ounces or a quarter, and slid into a paper bag. It seemed an ideal way for a kid to spend his pocket money (if he got any!).

Rolos were popular; their advert stated that they were 'tops in popularity' and showed a boy spinning a top (popular at the time) on a pack of Rolos. The slogan continued 'all the gang loves Mackintosh's Rolos'. Mars bars appeared in adverts in magazines with the caption 'stars love Mars because Mars are marvellous'. A popular advert showed Terry-Thomas munching on a Mars bar with the caption 'Mars fills the gap for me between meals' (the gap also referred to the gap in his front teeth!). The advert continued 'there's a fine How-d'ye-do if Terry-Thomas finds he's out of Mars – for Terry finds their mouth-watering goodness irresistible. More and more Mars is his motto – they're so marvellous! Everybody's favourite sweet treat and only 5*d*.' Cadbury's twopenny milk flakes were also popular, along with Cadbury's Dairy Milk chocolate, whose caption was 'taste the cream in Cadburys!'

Nestlé's Snap first came out in 1957. It included peanuts in crunchy brittle covered in milk chocolate, all for 4*d*! By saving the wrappers, you could enter competitions to win wonderful prizes such as Duaflex cameras and Newmark wristwatches. Everybody at the time pronounced Nestlé as 'nestle' and it would be decades later that people started saying 'nes-lay' instead!

Other confectionery included Bassett's Allsorts. Their advert read 'Bertie calling ... you can't resist them – they're inexpensive too – the good old British sweet the whole family enjoys.'

Also available was Walton's Palm Toffee ('The Perfection of Confections') and Caley Tray, which featured six different chocolates on every bar, including coffee cream, Turkish delight, gooseberry cream, caramel, praline pâté and nougat.

Boxes of chocolates for mums on birthdays (or when Dad had done something wrong!) included Cadbury's Milk Tray or perhaps Mackintosh's Quality Street.

Range Rider Lucky Bags cost 3*d* and were loved by kids. They included toys, games, puzzles, sweets and other items, like transfers and stickers. They were also known as Jamboree Bags and Pirate Bags. You never knew what you were going to get when you bought one, which made it all a bit more exciting. Many contained small soldiers, yo-yos, plastic spinning tops, whistles and colourful hairgrips.

Many chocolates and sweets were around for decades after, and some are still with us today, including Crunchie, KitKat, Aero, Toblerone, Caramac (which cost 6*d* at the time), Maltesers, Cadbury's Dairy Milk and Smarties (which always came in boxes).

Sweets like Spangles, Sky Bar, Punch and Crackerchoc have disappeared forever. However, Opal Fruits still survive today as Starburst.

Cadbury produced many popular chocolates and so did Fry's, who made Chocolate Creams, Turkish Delight, Five Centre and Peppermint Creams. Fry's were Cadbury's greatest rival and had been producing chocolate since 1866. Ironically, they are now owned by Cadbury!

Other well-liked chocolates and sweets included Murray Mints (the too good to hurry mints!), Rowntree's fruit gums, Waifa, Polo mints, Double Fruit, Cadbury's Fruit and Nut, Victory Jelly Babies, Raisin Block, Munchies, Picnic (which cost 6*d*) and Nestlé's hazelnut milk chocolate.

Even after the long rationing of the war years, many sweet manufacturers were soon back on their feet, and there was soon a wide variety of sweets and chocolates on the market, including many which are still fondly remembered.

7

Fashions

Clothes rationing had begun on 1 June 1941 and had continued until 15 March 1949. At the beginning of the 1950s, the 'make do and mend' ideal still continued. Clothes for children were much like the clothes that their parents wore. Boys wore flannel shorts down to their knees, no matter what the weather, with pulled-up socks, a shirt and knitted jumper. The jumper would always be knitted by someone in the family and certainly not machine-made or bought in a shop. Clothes and fashions of the day including knitted swimsuits, jumpers, gloves and bobble hats. All mothers knitted clothes for their children back then. Knitting was a popular pastime and was a way to make clothes cheaply for the whole family. Every corner shop and post office sold wool, and the sound of clicking needles could be heard everywhere – at home, on buses, in cinemas, etc. Seamstresses made their own clothes out of hand-me-down garments and any spare material.

Woolworths stocked a large selection of clothes patterns at 3d each, featuring modern styles to encourage mums to buy their wool, cotton and needles from the shop. Woolworths also stocked Ladybird clothing. Their aim at the time was to offer fashionable clothing at reasonable prices. By 1953, Woolworths offered a wide range of clothing, including knitted jumpers, blouses, shirts, school wear and casual wear for children. Sales of clothes at Woolworths rocketed in the 1950s as people strived to get away from the drab clothes of pre-war fashion and the rationing of the 1940s. Even so, it was still more common to see a child in a jumper knitted by his mum, or some other relation, than it was to see them in one from Woolworths!

Boys were expected to be neat and tidy, especially when going to school or church. Any special occasion meant a trip to the barber's, whether you needed a haircut or not. There was only one style for boys – short back and sides! Girls had their hair in ringlets or curls, produced by tying strips of rags in their hair when they went to bed. Mothers would perm their hair with pink and blue rollers, and use setting lotions to produce waves or curls. No appointments had to be made for boys or men at the barber's. You just went along and waited your turn while your dad read the newspaper. If there was someone in the chair, the barber would be talking about sport, mainly football, news or the weather.

Ladybird clothes were popular with young mums. Ladybird had been going since the 1950s and had a good relationship with Woolworths; the shop stocked brightly patterned T-shirts and jeans for children.

For many children, especially those with older brothers or sisters, clothes included many ill-fitting hand-me-downs. It was a time when there was little wastage, and most things were used time and time again until they fell apart. Many children hated their hand-me-down clothes, mainly because they were often too big.

Blakeys were used on shoes to stop the soles and heels wearing down so quickly. They were made of metal and were hammered into the back of your shoe. They had one drawback – the noise! Everyone could hear you coming with the click-click sound! They also ruined floors, and many schools eventually banned them.

Clarks shoes were well established by the 1950s and Tuf shoes came in in the later 1950s. Tuf shoes boasted that they didn't need repairing and came with a six-month guarantee. Vulcanised rubber soles were introduced, which gave the shoe a longer life. Some kids found them uncomfortable, though, and got blisters until they were 'broken in'. Many kids just went around in their black plimsolls most of the time.

In the later 1950s, winkle-pickers became very popular, but parents frowned on them being worn to school.

By 1953, Teddy boys had appeared on the streets of London. Their clothes were inspired by styles worn by previous generations in the Edwardian period. The way of dress soon spread across Great Britain and became strongly associated with the new craze of rock 'n' roll. They were originally known as Cosh boys. The name Teddy boy came from a headline in the *Daily Express* in 1953, which had shortened the word 'Edwardian' to 'Teddy'.

By the mid-1950s, with rock 'n' roll taking off, Teddy boys could be seen everywhere, complete with drainpipe trousers and long jackets with velvet collars. All had hair slicked back with Brylcreem in a DA style.

Fashions for adults changed greatly in the 1950s. Mass-produced ready-to-wear clothing became available. Women wore colourful dresses made of lighter material than that which had been seen in the war years. New materials had recently been invented, including Nylon, Crimplene and Orlon, and all were used extensively. They were all machine washable and reasonably priced. Women's fashion changed greatly during the 1950s and included casual, relaxed clothing, including button-up sweaters, full knee-length skirts and fitted blouses. Casual dresses included halter-necks, circle skirts or small collars. Fashions that took off in the 1950s included the trapeze dress and tunic-style suits worn with a slim skirt. Christian Dior and Coco Chanel both produced fashion lines popular with women in the 1950s.

Other fashionable items worn in the 1950s included, as mentioned before, winkle-pickers, a style of shoe or boot worn mainly by rock 'n' roll fans. They featured long pointed toes. Popular shoes for Teddy boys included brothel creepers, which featured crêpe soles. A pair of brothel creepers, drainpipe trousers, a draped jacket and bolo ties made up the uniform of the 1950s Teddy boy. Jackets were, in some cases, made of velvet, sometimes in bright electric blue or other loud colours. Together with a quiff or pompadour haircut, the look of the Teddy boy was complete.

The chances were that most children's parents in the 1950s probably weren't too affected by the fashions of the decade. Dad would have gone to work in a shirt and tie, trousers and jacket, perhaps with a cloth cap, and Mum would have had her ordinary clothes for around the house, with maybe a special suit of clothes for days out or evening wear for going to restaurants, etc. Teddy-boy clothes were mainly for the young, unmarried men who were into their image and enjoyed visiting milk bars; it would be very unlikely that anyone's dad would have picked them up from school dressed like that. Fashions come and go, and a lot of everyday people were untouched by the new crazes.

8

Radio

Today, it's hard to believe what an important part radio played in people's lives. For many years, before television, it was the main source of entertainment and news.

Most families at the beginning of the 1950s had radios, and families would gather around to listen to the latest programmes broadcast by the BBC. In the days before television became widely popular, it was one of the main forms of home entertainment. Even with the introduction of television, the radio remained immensely popular, with shows such as *Hancock's Half Hour*, *The Goons* and *The Archers*.

Hancock's Half Hour broke with the tradition of variety shows on the radio and became one of the first situation comedies broadcast. The cast consisted of Tony Hancock, Sidney James, Bill Kerr, Kenneth Williams, Hattie Jacques and Moira Lister.

Sidney James played 'Sid', the criminally inclined friend of Hancock, who each week usually conned him out of money; Bill Kerr played an Australian lodger; and Kenneth Williams, in his first comedy role, provided the voices for different minor characters each week.

Other notable actors who popped up in the series included John Le Mesurier, Hugh Lloyd, Dick Emery, Richard Wattis, Pat Coombs, Rolf Harris and Burt Kwouk (billed as 'Burd Kwouk').

Most of the action took place at Hancock's home at 23 Railway Cuttings, East Cheam. The show was written by Ray Galton and Alan Simpson, and became immensely popular, being transferred to television in 1956.

Similar shows included *A Life of Bliss* starring George Cole. *Life with the Lyons* starred a real-life American family, consisting of Ben Lyon and his wife Bebe Daniels. It was scripted but featured real-life events. It ran from 1955 until 1960.

The Goon Show was broadcast from 1951 until 1960 by the BBC Home Service. The first series, broadcast in 1951, was called *Crazy People* but later series were renamed *The Goon Show*, which was the idea of Spike Milligan who was a fan of *Popeye* – a character called Alice the Goon appeared in the *Popeye* comic strips and cartoons. The show featured Milligan, as well as Peter Sellers, Harry Secombe and Michael Bentine. Milligan himself was the show's creator, and wrote most of the shows. The show involved ludicrous plots, surreal humour, strange voices and weird electronic noises, which were created by the then-new BBC Radiophonic Workshop. The show was broadcast all over the world to countries including Australia, New Zealand, South Africa, India and Canada. It had a major effect on later comedy, especially *Monty Python's Flying Circus*.

Dick Barton, Special Agent ran from 1946 to 1951 and was broadcast daily by the BBC. It aired at 6.45 p.m. every evening on weekdays, and was incredibly popular, with a peak audience of 15 million listeners. It featured the adventures of ex-Commando Richard Barton MC. With his associates Jock Anderson and Snowy White, he solved crimes and saved the nation from disaster. The show was essential teatime listening. Although extremely popular, the show was cancelled the following year after *The Archers* began to be broadcast. It was felt that the new programme was more suitable listening for a post-war audience, although it never achieved the popularity of *Dick Barton*, which was much missed when it ended.

The Archers was originally listed as 'an everyday story of country folk', and still continues today, making it the world's longest-running radio soap. Set in the fictional village of Ambridge, it told the story of the middle-class farming family, the Archers. It was first broadcast on Whit Monday on 29 May 1950, with five episodes being transmitted throughout the week. The pilot series, created by Godfrey Baseley, was described as 'a farming Dick Barton'.

Educating Archie was a BBC Light Programme that was broadcast from June 1950 until February 1958. It featured Peter Brough and his ventriloquist doll Archie Andrews. The show ran on Sunday lunchtimes and had a listenership of 15 million. A fan club was set up which had 250,000 members. The comedy worked well on radio, although it seemed odd having a ventriloquist whom nobody could see. The show was so popular that it won the *Daily Mail*'s Variety Award just four months after it started. The show also featured many famous comedians, including Benny Hill, Tony Hancock, Harry Secombe, Dick Emery, Bernard Bresslaw and Bruce Forsyth. Julie Andrews played Archie's girlfriend. The show transferred to television in 1958, but in truth Peter Brough wasn't such a great ventriloquist. However, it was still well received.

Paul Temple was created by Francis Durbridge for the BBC and featured in their serial, *Send for Paul Temple*, in 1938. Temple was a private eye who, together with his journalist wife Louise (known as 'Steve' after her pen name 'Steve Trent'), solved whodunnit-type crimes with humour and plenty of action. The character also appeared in a comic strip in the *London Evening Standard* during the 1950s. In the early 1950s radio shows, Kim Peacock played Paul Temple and Marjory Westbury played Steve. From 1954 onwards, Paul Coke played Temple.

Beyond Our Ken was broadcast between 1958 and 1964 and starred Kenneth Horne, together with Kenneth Williams, Hugh Paddick, Betty Marsden and Bill Pertwee. The show's announcer was Douglas Smith. The scripts were written by Eric Merriman and Barry Took. The comedy series was a forerunner to *Round the Horne* (1965–68). Favourite characters in the show included Hankie Flowered (Bill Pertwee parodying Frankie Howerd), Betty Marsden's Fanny Haddock (based on Fanny Craddock) and Ricky Livid played by Hugh Paddick, who was sending up stars of the day such as Marty Wilde and Billy Fury.

Journey into Space was a science-fiction show written by BBC producer Charles Chilton. It was the last radio programme to attract a larger evening audience than television. Four series were produced and it was broadcast worldwide. Chilton wrote three best-selling novels and several comic strips based on the show. It was first broadcast in 1953 and featured four main characters including Captain Andrew 'Jet' Morgan, Doc Matthews, Stephen 'Mitch' Mitchell and Lemuel 'Lemmy' Barnet. Many actors played the main parts, including Ed Bishop (later seen in *UFO*), David Kossoff, Alfie Bass, Deryck Guyler, Andrew Faulds and David Jacobs. The three original series were entitled *Journey to the Moon/Operation Luna*, *The Red Planet* and *The World in Peril*. Originally, the first series was just entitled *Journey into Space*, but within the BBC was known as *Journey to the Moon*. It was set in the future in the year 1965 – it was believed that man would have walked on the moon by then. The first episode attracted 5.1 million listeners but the further earthbound episodes only attracted 4 million. When the rocket set off for the moon in the fifth episode, the audience numbers grew immensely. The series was extended to eighteen episodes, and by the time it had finished over 8 million people were tuning in. The second series, *The Red Planet* (broadcast in 1954), followed the further adventures of the crew as they tried to reach and explore Mars. The third series, *The World in Peril* (broadcast in 1955), saw Jet Morgan and his crew returning to Mars to try and halt an alien invasion.

The Billy Cotton Band Show ran from 1949 to 1968 and was broadcast on Sunday afternoons. Cotton would start the show by shouting, 'Wakey-Wake-aaaay!' followed by 'Somebody Stole My Gal', the band's signature tune. Regular entertainers on the show included pianist Russ Conway, Alan Breeze, Kathy Kay and Doreen Stephens. Michael Palin and Terry Jones wrote many jokes for the show.

Children's Favourites was first broadcast in 1954 and featured requests from children of all ages. It was broadcast on Sunday mornings at 9 a.m. and was introduced by Derek McCulloch, who was known as Uncle Mac. He opened the show with 'Hello children, everywhere' and ended it with 'Goodnight children, everywhere', which became his catchphrase. The theme song to the show was 'Puffin Billy' played by the Melodi Light Orchestra. Many children wrote in just to hear their names on the radio. McCulloch made his last broadcast in 1965 and eventually the show was renamed *Junior Choice*.

The Clitheroe Kid ran between 1957 and 1972 and featured the diminutive Northern comedian Jimmy Clitheroe. In the show he played the part of a cheeky schoolboy who lived with his family at 33 Lilac Avenue. The show also featured Patricia Burke as his mother, Peter Sinclair as his Scottish grandad, Diana Day as his sister Susan (the part was also played by Judith Chalmers), Danny Ross played Alfie Hall (Susan's boyfriend), and Tony Melody played Mr Higginbottom. Clitheroe was thirty-five when he first took the part but could pass for a eleven-year-old boy because of his small stature. Even when recording the show, Clitheroe would wear a school blazer and cap. The programme was immensely popular with radio listeners at the time.

Does the Team Think? was a panel game which ran from 1957 to 1976. It was revived in 2007. It was a send-up of the show *Any Questions?* and the audience would ask the panel questions, to which they would reply with witty answers. In the 1950s, the panel was chaired by McDonald Hobley, and regular panel members included Arthur Askey and Ted Ray.

Friday Night Is Music Night was first broadcast in 1952, and is the world's longest-running live concert programme. It featured a range of music including classical, film, swing, jazz, opera, folk and songs from musicals.

Housewives' Choice ran from 1946 to 1967, and was a request show playing music that would appeal to housewives at home during the day. It featured mainly pop music of the day and achieved huge audiences. The theme tune was 'In the Party Mood' by Jack Strachey. There were various presenters but one of the most popular was George Elrick, who would sing his own lyrics over the theme song.

Listen With Mother ran between 1950 and 1982. It was broadcast every weekday afternoon at 1.45 p.m. and lasted fifteen minutes. Its presenters included Daphne Oxenford, Eileen Brown, Julia Lang, Dorothy Smith and many others. It consisted of stories, nursery rhymes and songs, which were regularly sung by Eileen Browne and George Dixon. The show was aimed at the under-fives and regularly had over 1 million listeners. The theme tune was Gabriel Fauré's 'Dolly Suite' and the show began with the words 'Are you sitting comfortably? Then I'll begin.' It led on to the television version, *Watch with Mother*.

Mrs Dale's Diary ran from 1948 until 1969. The story revolved around Mrs Mary Dale who was a doctor's wife living at Virginia Lodge in the fictional middle-class area of Parkwood Hill. The main scriptwriter was Jonqil Antony and he was joined by Ted Willis, who would later write for *Dixon of Dock Green*. Until 1963, Mrs Dale was played by Ellis Powell before being replaced by Jessie Matthews. Each episode would begin with a brief narrative by Mrs Dale, as if she were reading from her diary. The show became one of the BBC's most popular serial dramas.

Much Binding in the Marsh was a comedy broadcast by both the BBC and Radio Luxembourg. It starred Kenneth Horne and Richard Murdoch as senior staff at an RAF station dealing with red tape and wartime matters. Other members of the cast included Sam Costa, Maurice Denham, Maureen Riscoe, Nicholas Parsons and Dora Bryan. Occasionally, the cast were joined by special guest stars, one of whom was Alan Ladd. The show was broadcast between 1944 and 1954; it switched to Radio Luxembourg in 1950 before returning back to the BBC in 1952.

Music While You Work was a live programme broadcast to entertain workers. It began in June 1940 and ended in September 1967. The show began during wartime, and it was thought that playing continuous popular music would help factory workers become more productive. Originally, the show consisted of live music from bands playing brass, dance, military and light music.

The Navy Lark was a very popular sitcom which revolved around life on a Naval ship, HMS *Troutbridge*. The main stars of the show were Jon Pertwee, Leslie Phillips and Stephen Murray. Other notable members of the cast included Ronnie Barker, Dennis Price, Richard Caldicott and Michael Bates. The show revolved around the mischief that Sub-Lt Phillips, Chief Petty Officer Pertwee and Lt Murray found themselves in, and their struggle to keep it from reaching the attention of their superior, Commander 'Thunderguts' Povey.

Pick of the Pops was originally broadcast in 1955 and was based on the UK's top twenty singles chart. Original presenters included Franklin Engelmann, Alan Dell and David Jacobs. It didn't feature the actual chart until September 1957, when Alan Dell played the charts from various music papers.

Ray's A Laugh was a comedy, set in a domestic situation, which starred Ted Ray. Kitty Bluett was played by his wife and Fred Yule played his brother-in-law. Also appearing in the series were Patricia Hayes and Kenneth Connor (as Sidney Mincing). Other actors who appeared included Peter Sellers, Pat Coombs, and Percy Edwards as Gregory the chicken. The show ran from 1949 until 1961.

Sing Something Simple ran from 1959 to 2001 and featured Cliff Adams and the Cliff Adams Singers. The lyrics to the main theme went

> Sing something simple
> As cares go by
> Sing something simple
> Just you and I

Take It from Here was a radio comedy show broadcast by the BBC between 1948 and 1960. It was written by Denis Norden and Frank Muir, and starred Jimmy Edwards, Dick Bentley and Joy Nichols. Nichols was later replaced by June Whitfield and Alma Cogan. The show was famous for introducing *The Glums*. The show included sketches, music and a discussion, and parodied popular films and books of the day. *The Glums* featured Jimmy Edwards as Mr Glum; his dim-witted son Ron, played by Dick Bentley; and Eth, Ron's long-term fiancée (played by June Whitfield).

Radio Luxembourg first began broadcasting in 1933 and was the forerunner to pirate radio. It allowed products to be advertised freely, which got around legislation in the UK, where the BBC had a monopoly and no advertising was allowed. The station became hugely popular in the 1950s, but could only be heard satisfactorily after dark.

Some of the popular shows during the 1950s included *The Ovaltiney's Concert Party*, broadcast at 6.15 p.m. on Sundays. The show had previously been transmitted before the war.

Other Sunday shows included *Leslie Welch, the Famous Memory Man* at 9.15 p.m., *The Answer Man: 'Anything You Want to Know'* at 10.45 p.m. (also broadcast on Wednesdays and Fridays) and the *Top Twenty with Pete Murray* at 11 p.m.

On Mondays at 7.15 p.m. there was *The Adventures of Dan Dare 'Pilot of the Future'*, which was a fifteen-minute serial that was also heard on other weekdays. It featured the voice of Noel Johnson, who also played the part of Dick Barton on the BBC. The show began in 1951 and ran for five years. Perry Mason was at 9.30 p.m. and also was broadcast every weekday.

On Tuesdays, the programmes featured *Soccer of Leicester* at 10.55 p.m.

The Story of Dr Kildare was featured every Wednesday at 8.30 p.m. It starred Lew Ayres and was produced in Hollywood by MGM.

On Thursdays, there was *Music from the Ballet* at 8 p.m., *Movie Magazine with Wilfrid Thomas* at 8.30 p.m., and *Old Fashioned Revival Hour* at 11 p.m., featuring religion with Charles E. Fuller.

Friday's shows included *Scottish Requests with Peter Madren* at 8 p.m. and *The Voice of Prophecy* (an Adventists' religious show) at 11 p.m.

Saturday's shows included *Chance of a Lifetime* at 7 p.m., which was a quiz programme hosted by Dick Emery. At 10 p.m. there was *At Two-O-Eight*, which featured dance music played by the Russ Morgan Orchestra. The show was hosted by Pete Murray. At 11 p.m. was *Bring Christ to the Nations*, which was the Lutheran hour.

Radio Luxembourg became a haven for stars who had fallen out with the BBC for one reason or another. When the

BBC wanted Vera Lynn to sing more upbeat songs, she left and signed to Radio Luxembourg in 1951, where she was allowed to sing her own style of music and was better paid. The comedy *Much Binding in the Marsh* also cropped up on Luxembourg after its contract was terminated in 1950.

Some of the shows listed in December 1956 included:

Sundays: 6 p.m. – *Butlin's Beaver Club* with Uncle Eric Winstone.

8.30 p.m. – *Take Your Pick* with Michael Miles.

9.30 p.m. –*This I Believe – The Edward R. Murrow Show* presented by Sir Basil Bartlett.

Mondays: 9.30 p.m. – *Candid Microphone* starring listeners caught in the act.

11.15 p.m. – *Frank and Ernest* religion from the Dawn Bible Students Association.

11.30 p.m. – *The World Tomorrow* with Herbert W. Armstrong, later heard on Tuesdays as well, replacing Oral Roberts.

Tuesdays: 9.00 p.m. – *Lucky Number* with Keith Fordyce.

10.00 p.m. – *The Capitol Show* – Mel Thompson presenting Capitol Records new releases.

Wednesdays: 8.00 p.m. – *Double Your Money* with Hughie Green.

10.00 p.m. – *Rockin' To Dreamland* with Keith Fordyce playing the latest British and American hit records.

11.30 p.m – *The Hour of Decision* with Billy Graham.

Thursdays: 8.30 p.m. – *Lucky Couple* with David Jacobs, recorded on location in the UK.

9.30 p.m. – *Irish Requests*.

10.45 p.m. – *Italy Sings* presented by the Italian State Tourist Office.

Fridays: 10.30 p.m. – *Record Hop* – Benny Lee presents the latest Columbia and Parlophone records.

Saturdays: 7.00 p.m. – *Amateur Football* – results of the matches played today.

8.00 p.m. – *Jamboree* – 120 minutes of exciting, non-stop, action-packed radio, *Teenage Jury* and at approximately 9.30 Alan Freed, the remarkable American disc jockey whose programmes in the States cause excitement to rise to a fever pitch, presents *Rock 'n' roll*.

10.00 p.m. – *Tonight* – Peter Haigh presents news, music and personalities recorded at the Embassy Club in London.

10.30 p.m. – *Philips' Fanfare* – records from this label presented by Guy Standeven.

By this time, many listeners had been lost to the new draw of the television set. Popular presenters of the 1950s included Barry Alldis, Chris Denning, Colin Hamilton, Ted King, Johnny Moran, Don Moss and Don Wardell. Other disc jockeys who appeared on the programme recorded their shows in London at Radio Luxembourg's studio at 38 Hertford Street. Many programmes were sponsored by record companies. The shows' hosts included Peter Aldersley, Sam Costa, Alan Dell, Keith Fordyce, Alan Freeman, David Gell, Tony Hall, Jack Jackson, David Jacobs, Brian Matthew, Don Moss, Pete Murray, Ray Orchard, Jimmy Savile, Shaw Taylor, Jimmy Young and Muriel Young.

9

Television

Television had been broadcast by the BBC since 1936, although few people had television sets. The coronation of Queen Elizabeth II on 2 June 1953 led to a huge rush to buy television sets. For the first time, cameras were allowed into Westminster Abbey and the whole event was broadcast live. Families and neighbours crowded around their small television sets to watch the event.

At first, there was only one channel, but in 1955 ITV was launched.

Popular shows on the television at the time included *Bilko, Ivanhoe, Six Five Special, Muffin the Mule, Crackerjack, Dixon of Dock Green, The Adventures of Robin Hood, William Tell, Sooty, Opportunity Knocks, Oh Boy!, Watch with Mother*, etc.

Watch with Mother was first broadcast in 1952, although many families didn't have a television set at the time. Programmes included *Andy Pandy, The Flower Pot Men, Picture Book* and *Rag, Tag and Bobtail*. By 1955, when most families now had televisions, *The Woodentops* was added to the series of shows broadcast. Originally broadcast at 3.45 p.m. and 4 p.m., it found its regular slot in 1955 and was broadcast each day at 1.30 p.m. with the programmes rotated in sequence. *Andy Pandy* had first appeared on British television in 1950 as part of the BBC's

'For the Children' series. *Andy Pandy* was a string puppet who lived in a wicker basket and was joined by Teddy and Looby Loo. When Andy and Teddy weren't around, Looby Loo would appear. She had her own song, 'Here we go Looby Loo!' The show would finish with:

Time to go home,
Time to go home,
Andy is waving goodbye.

The shows were originally broadcast live but the decision was made to film them so that they could be regularly repeated. There was also a comic-strip version of Andy which featured in the weekly children's magazine *Robin*. Andy Pandy was said to be based on the son of the puppeteer, Audrey Atterbury.

The Flower Pot Men featured Bill and Ben and their adventures in an English garden. The series was devised by Freda Lingstrom and Maria Bird. The puppeteers were again Audrey Atterbury joined by Molly Gibson. The voices were supplied by Peter Hawkins, Gladys Whitred and Julia Williams. One of the show's devisors, Maria Bird, provided the narration. Bill and Ben would appear at the beginning of the show and would be joined by Little Weed. Their voices were unique and included words like 'loblob' (lovely) and 'flobberpop' (flowerpot). Both were voiced by Peter Hawkins. Some viewers felt that the voices hindered children from talking properly, but it was incredibly popular and was probably the favourite *Watch with Mother* show.

The Woodentops was created by Freda Lingstrom and Maria Bird, and featured a family of wooden dolls that lived on a farm. These included Daddy Woodentop, Mummy Woodentop, Jenny Woodentop, Willy Woodentop and Baby Woodentop. Other characters included Spotty Dog, 'the very biggest spotty dog you ever did see', Buttercup the cow, and Mrs Scrubbitt and Sam Scrubbitt, who helped around the farm.

Apart from *Watch with Mother*, other popular children's programmes included *The Adventures of Noddy*, which first aired in 1955. It again featured Peter Hawkins who did the voices of both Big Ears and Mr Plod. *Captain Pugwash* was first shown on the BBC in 1957 and was broadcast live using cardboard cut-outs. The show was produced by Gordon Murray. The voices were again provided by Peter Hawkins.

Captain Horatio Pugwash originally featured in the first issue of *The Eagle* in 1950 before appearing in a comic strip in the *Radio Times*. Characters featured aboard the *Black Pig* included Master Mate, Barnabas, Willy, Tom the Cabin Boy and Cut-Throat Jake.

The Adventures of Twizzle was a fifteen-minute puppet show which was shown on ITV from 1957 until 1962. There were fifty-two episodes, which were directed by Gerry Anderson and made by AP Films. The programme featured Twizzle, a doll who had escaped from a toy shop. His subsequent adventures also featured Footso the cat. AP Films had been newly formed by Gerry Anderson, Arthur Provis, Reg Hill and Sylvia Tamm, and *The Adventures of Twizzle* was its first production. They had originally set up the company to make films for the cinema but there was little work, and when they were approached by author Roberta Leigh they accepted her offer to make fifty-two shows featuring Twizzle. They weren't particularly happy about making a show featuring puppets but, with rising debts, took on the work. Twizzle's reason for running away from the toyshop was because he didn't want to be bought by a particularly nasty girl. His extendable arms played a major part in each show, such as in the episode when he rescues Chawky, a white-faced golliwog, who inflates his bicycle tyres too much and begins to float away. Amazingly, for all its simplicity, the show was a huge success. It aired between 6 p.m. and 7 p.m. It was the beginning of fame and fortune for AP Films and Gerry Anderson, and just seven years later they made the incredibly successful television show *Thunderbirds*.

Hergé's *Adventures of Tintin* aired from 1958 onwards. It featured cartoon adaptations of the comic strips and was produced by Belvision. The main characters were Tintin (a young Belgian reporter), Snowy (his white fox terrier), Captain Haddock (Tintin's best friend), Professor Calculus (an absent-minded professor), and many supporting characters, including Thompson and Thompson (two bumbling detectives), Bianca Castafiore (an opera singer whom Captain Haddock despises) and many other recurring characters, such as Nestor the butler and Chang the loyal Chinese boy.

Popular adult shows also enjoyed by children included *Ivanhoe* with Roger Moore. It was first shown on ITV between 1958 and 1959. Moore played Sir Wilfred of Ivanhoe and the show featured characters loosely based on Sir Walter Scott's 1819 novel. The show was set in the twelfth century during the reign of King Richard the Lionheart. While Richard was away fighting the Crusades, the evil Prince John ruled, and Ivanhoe, with his companions Gurth and Bart, helped the needy and tried to right wrongs. The series stoked children's imaginations and they re-enacted scenes in the woods or nearby playing fields. Another popular series that had the same effect was *The Adventures of Robin Hood*, which featured Richard Greene as Robin Hood. Alan Wheatley played his nemesis, the Sheriff of Nottingham. The programme was shown weekly between 1955 and 1959 on ITV. Many boys set off to the woods after seeing the show and made their own bows and arrows from a few branches and a piece of string. The show proved incredibly popular and was sold to America where it aired on the CBS channel. The show featured Robin, Maid Marion and the Merry Men, which included Little John, Friar Tuck, Will Scarlet and Alan-a-Dale. Many famous faces later popped up in the show including Patrick Troughton, Lionel Jeffries, Sam Kydd, Sid James, Jane Asher, Leslie Philips, Harry H. Corbett, Leo McKern and Bernard Bresslaw.

The theme song was written by Carl Sigman and was sung by Dick James. It was very catchy and is well remembered. It was sung by children all over Britain as they re-enacted scenes from their favourite show. The words were:

Robin Hood! Robin Hood! Riding through the glen!
Robin Hood! Robin Hood! With his band of men!
Feared by the bad! Loved by the good!
Robin Hood! Robin Hood! Robin Hood!
He called the greatest archers to a tavern on the green!
They vowed to help the people of the king!
They handled all the trouble on the English country scene!
And still found plenty of time to sing!
Robin Hood! Robin Hood! Riding through the glen!
Robin Hood! Robin Hood! With his band of men!
Feared by the bad! Loved by the good!
Robin Hood! Robin Hood! Robin Hood!

The Adventures of William Tell was another children's favourite and many kids tried to shoot apples off their pals' heads in the nearby woods. The show aired on ITV in 1958 and starred Conrad Phillips in the lead role. The show also starred Jennifer Jayne as Hedda Tell (his wife), Richard Rogers as Walter Tell (his son), Nigel Green as The Bear and Jack Lambert as Judge Furst. It was made at Elstree and outdoor shots of lakes and hills were filmed at Snowdonia in Wales. The theme song was the *William Tell Overture* by Rossini.

All these shows fired a child's imagination and included much fighting and swashbuckling.

Another popular show to use Rossini's *William Tell Overture* was *The Lone Ranger*, which aired throughout the 1950s. Westerns were very popular at the time, both on the television and in the cinema. The show starred Clayton Moore as the Lone Ranger and Jay Silverheels as Tonto (his Red Indian sidekick). Westerns played a major part in television shows in the 1950s, and other popular ones, all made in America, included *Gunsmoke* (with James Arness), *The Rifleman* (starring Chuck Connors), *Wanted: Dead or Alive* (with Steve McQueen), *Laramie* (with John Smith), *Have Gun – Will Travel* (with Richard Boone), *Bonanza* (with Lorne Greene), *Wagon Train* (with Ward Bond), *Maverick* (with James Garner), *Sugarfoot* (with Will Hutchins) and *Cheyenne* (with Clint Walker). There were many, many more. All fuelled the imaginations of children, who re-enacted scenes in the streets, some with cowboy outfits and many with guns that fired caps. Westerns remained popular on television throughout the 1950s until the mid-1970s.

Another popular import from America was *The Phil Silvers Show*, which was more popularly known as *Sergeant Bilko*. Silvers played Master Sergeant Ernest G. Bilko and each week he would be seen trying to pull a scam or get one over on someone.

It was set at the army base at Fort Baxter in Roseville, Kansas. The story revolved around the soldiers of the Fort Baxter motor pool, who were commanded by Bilko and aided his regular scams and get-rich-quick schemes.

The show was originally filmed in front of a live audience, which produced lots of laughs, especially when some of the cast forgot their lines. Other popular characters that appeared in the show were Private Duane Doberman (Maurice Gosfield), Corporal Rocco Barbella (Harvey Lembeck), Corporal Steve Henshaw (Allan Melvin) and

Bilko's long-suffering superior Colonel John T. Hall (Paul Ford). The show proved a huge success both in America and the UK. The later cartoon series *Top Cat* took much from Bilko, including the voices.

Before Your Very Eyes was a sketch-based show, featuring Arthur Askey, which aired on the BBC between 1952 and 1955 before transferring over to ITV between 1956 and 1958. Askey had been a popular radio and cinema star, and transferred to television with ease. His catchphrases, 'ay thang yew!' and 'hello, playmates!' (as well as many others), were known and were regularly repeated all over the land at the time.

A popular children's comedy was *Billy Bunter of Greyfriars School*, which featured Gerald Campion as the greedy, overweight main character. The show aired on the BBC between 1952 and 1961. The show also featured Kynaston Reeves and Frank Melford as Mr Quelch. Frank Richards' stories about Billy Bunter first appeared in the *Magnet* comic in 1908 and continued weekly until it ceased publication in 1940. Bunter was one of a class of boys known as 'The Remove' and he was known as 'the fat owl of the Remove'. Other pupils included Bob Cherry, Harry Wharton, Frank Nugent, Johnny Bull, and an Indian boy Hurree Singh, who had the nickname 'Inky'. The plots revolved around Bunter's attempts to get more tuck, which included jam tarts and doughnuts. The other boys continually poked fun at both his size and greed, although there were no complaints from viewers about their continued bullying. Amazingly, Gerald Campion was thirty-two years old when he first played Billy Bunter, and he continued with the role until he was forty. Among the teenage television actors playing his classmates were David Hemmings, Melvyn Hayes, Michael Crawford and Anthony Valentine.

The Black and White Minstrel Show first aired on the BBC in 1958 and amazingly continued until 1978, before being axed because it was considered racist. The show's regular cast included the Mitchell Minstrels, the Television Toppers, Tony Mercer, Dai Francis and John Boulter, with compères George Chisholm, Stan Stennett, Leslie Crowther and Don Maclean. The show featured white male singers, with their faces blackened, singing songs from America's Deep South. It first appeared as a one-off special, *The 1957 Television Minstrels*, and featured the all-male Mitchell Minstrels. Although it certainly wouldn't be made today, *The Black and White Minstrel Show* was tremendously popular at the time and even won the Golden Rose of Montreux in 1961.

The Buccaneers was a show about pirates which starred Robert Shaw as Dan Tempest. It was made by Sapphire Films for ITV and first aired in 1956, continuing until 1957. The thirty-nine episodes lasted thirty minutes each and were directed by Ralph Smart and Leslie Arliss. It also featured Paul Hansard as Taffy/Alfie, Peter Hammond as Lt Beamish, Edwin Richfield as Armando, Alec Clunes as Governor Woodes Rogers, Neil Hallett as Sam Bassett/Hornigold and Brian Rawlinson as Gaff/Davies. The low budget meant that many of the supporting actors appeared in two roles. *The Buccaneers* told the story of a pirate and his crew aboard *The Sultana*. It was set in the Bahamas in the early 1700s and the opening episode featured the governor, Woodes Rogers (played by Alec Clunes), offering all pirates a free pardon, which many accepted. The villain of the piece is Blackbeard (played by George Margo) who refuses the king's pardon. His character recurs throughout the series and there is much swashbuckling, although, probably due to budget, the buccaneers were often land-based.

Dixon of Dock Green featured Jack Warner in the title role. His character had been killed off in the film *The Blue Lamp* but was resurrected for the television series. It first aired in July 1955 and continued until 1976.

1. The pre-decimalisation coins used in the 1950s, including two shillings, a half crown, a halfpenny, a farthing, a threepenny bit, a sixpence and a penny. Money went much further in the 1950s, and most children were quite happy to be given pennies when they toured the streets on Guy Fawkes Night asking 'Penny for the Guy?'

Above left: 2. Most houses in the 1950s didn't have fitted baths or central heating so tin baths were used. The best place to sit in the bath, to keep warm, was in front of a roaring coal fire in the kitchen.

Above right: 3. Tri-ang tin pedal cars were much sought after by small boys, who would later go on to construct their own go-karts from spare wood and discarded pram wheels.

Above left: 4. Boys loved to emulate the boxers of the day, including Henry Cooper, and would get gloves for Christmas or birthdays.

Above right: 5. Every boy and girl wanted their own bike. Many were second-hand or built by their dads, but that didn't stop the enjoyment of riding them around the streets.

Below right: 6. Playing with toy cars was much enjoyed, especially by boys.

Opposite bottom: 7. Christmas morning was perhaps the most exciting day of the year for young children, and was much anticipated. The excitement of waking up to find lots of presents, left by Santa during the night, started off the perfect day, which would include Christmas dinner, games and other activities.

Above: 8. Corgi Toys advert.

Opposite top left: 9. There was much fun to be had at Christmas dinner. Apart from a meal of turkey, Yorkshire pudding and vegetables, as well as Christmas pudding, there was also the fun of pulling Christmas crackers and playing games afterwards.

Opposite top right: 10. The only holidays that some children would have would be day trips to the seaside by train. There was still much fun to be had: building sandcastles, walking along the pier, playing on slot machines and eating candy floss.

Opposite bottom: 11. The excitement of knowing that Santa had visited in the night meant that most children couldn't wait to get out of bed and open their presents.

Above: 14. An advert for Corgi Toys, which rivalled Matchbox and Dinky. Corgi were advertised as 'the ones with windows'. The Landrover model sold for 3s 6d.

Opposite top: 12. Every boy loved going on boat trips, whether it was going out fishing or just for a holiday cruise around the bay.

Opposite bottom: 13. The joy of opening presents on Christmas morning. This present reveals a toy cowboy cap gun.

15. Most young children of the 1950s yearned to be outside playing football or other games with their friends.

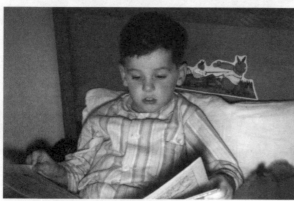

16. Every child enjoyed reading, or being read to, in bed before they went to sleep for the night.

Opposite top: 18. A grandad and his grandson, complete with cowboy outfit and cap gun. Cowboy films and television programmes were immensely popular with boys, who would re-enact mock battles in the street or in nearby woods or playing fields. *The Lone Ranger*, starring Clayton Moore, was incredibly popular, as was *Davy Crockett, King of the Wild Frontier*.

Opposite bottom: 19. Playing with cars on Christmas morning.

Left: 17. On a swing being pushed by Dad.

"The Bristolian" fastest regular train in the country...

now in a *new* Hornby-Dublo set

Here's a fine new model. This latest Hornby-Dublo electric train set is a splendid representation of "The Bristolian" pulled by one of the famous Castle class locomotives "Bristol Castle". It's in true Western Region colours with all the detail you could wish for . . . copper-capped chimney; correctly tapered boiler; name plates; brassed beadings and a host of other details that will please you, all true to the original. You'll be proud to own this superb Hornby-Dublo model.

Available now—see it at your dealers, or write for the latest colour folder to Dept. B.P.2, Meccano Limited, Binns Road, Liverpool 13 ; or to the London Showrooms at 22 Berkeley Square, W.I.

MECCANO LIMITED
BINNS ROAD
LIVERPOOL 13

HORNBY DUBLO ELECTRIC TRAINS

20. Advert for Hornby Dublo train set.

21. Having fun on a bicycle in the yard.

22. A day out to the seaside could include a ride on a donkey or pony. Many adults visiting the beach just wore their everyday clothes with perhaps their trouser legs or shirt sleeves rolled up.

23. A Christmas meal at home, complete with party hats and Christmas crackers.

Above: 25. The cast of the annual school nativity play. There would be much excitement, both from pupils and their parents, when the school nativity play was performed. It was all part of the lead up to a child's favourite time of year – Christmas!

Left: 26. A typical school photograph. The school photographers would visit the school and take photographs of the pupils, which could then be bought by their parents.

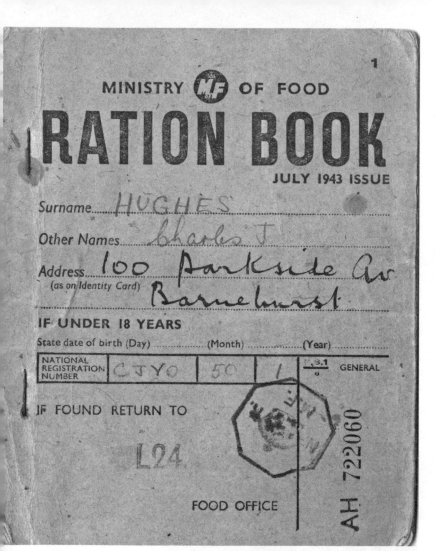

MINISTRY **MF** OF FOOD

RATION BOOK

JULY 1943 ISSUE

Surname ___HUGHES___

Other Names ___Charles J___

Address ___100 Parkside Av___
(as on Identity Card) ___Barnehurst___

IF UNDER 18 YEARS

State date of birth (Day) _____ (Month) _____ (Year) _____

NATIONAL REGISTRATION NUMBER	CJYO	50	1	3.1	GENERAL

IF FOUND RETURN TO

L24

FOOD OFFICE

AH. 722060

27. Rationing continued after the Second World War and didn't come to an end until
July 1954.

Opposite top: 24. Day trips to the zoo or circus were very exciting for young
children and would be talked about for days after with their friends at school.

28. On the beach with Mum and ice cream.

29. At a model village with Gran and Grandad.

30. There was much fun to be had at the local park, where there were no worries about health and safety, and children often came home with grazed arms or knees from playing on the swings, see-saw or slide.

31. Knocking out Dad with a new set of boxing gloves. Boxing was one of the sports participated in at school, much to the dismay of many of its pupils but seemingly to the delight of the PT teacher!

32. Playing with toy cowboys. Every boy loved cowboys in the 1950s, mainly because of the many films and television shows. Also in this picture is a Lego set, a *Wagon Train* annual and a 'Magic Slate', which allowed you to write and then erase what you had written.

33. With Mum in a Tri-ang tin car.

CLOTHING BOOK

1945-46
GENERAL CB 1/8

This book must not be used until the holder's name, full postal address and National Registration Number have been written below. Detach this book at once and keep it safely. It is your only means of buying clothing.

HOLDER'S NAME __HUGHES   CJ__
(in BLOCK letters)

ADDRESS __100 Parllside Avenue__
(in BLOCK letters) __Barnehurst S1.__

HOLDER'S NATIONAL REGISTRATION No.
__CJVO/ 50/ 1__

IF FOUND please take this book to any Food Office or Police Station

FOOD OFFICE CODE No.

L.34

THIS BOOK IS NUMBER

K 566714

HOLD Pages I—VIII in one hand and
TEAR ALONG THIS LINE

PAGE I

34. Although clothes rationing had ended in 1949, people still had the 'make do and mend' attitude, and this continued well into the 1950s.

Other cast members were Peter Byrne as Detective Sergeant Andy Crawford, Billie Whitelaw, Jeannette Hutchinson, Anna Dawson as Mary Crawford, Geoffrey Adams as Detective Constable Lauderdale, Arthur Rigby as Desk Sgt Flint, Nicholas Donnelly as PC Willis, Anthony Parker as PC Bob Penney and Jocelyne Rhodes as WPC Kay Shaw. George Dixon was a typical 'bobby-on-the-beat' in a time when policemen were a more common sight patrolling the streets. Each episode began with the character talking straight to the camera and with what was to become Dixon's catchphrase: 'Evening all'. In its heyday, the show attracted over 14 million viewers and Warner was eighty years old when he finally gave up the role in 1976. It was an easy-going police drama with simple tales of petty theft and other crimes, but was incredibly popular in its day.

Quiz shows offering cash prizes arrived on the television in 1955. The first, shown on the newly formed ITV, was *Double Your Money*, which was hosted by Hughie Green. The show had previously been featured on Radio Luxembourg before being transferred to television. Contestants answered a series of questions, which became harder as the show went on. The first question answered would win them £1 and their prize money was doubled each time they got a correct answer. Once they reached £32, they had the choice of returning the next week to play for the Treasure Trail, which could lead to the ultimate jackpot of £1,000. Questions, once the contestant had won £32, were asked in an isolation booth so that they could concentrate and also so they didn't hear the answers shouted by the live audience.

Previously, the BBC had transmitted panel shows such as *What's My Line* (1951–62) and *Animal, Vegetable, Mineral?* (1952–59), but shows like *Double Your Money* and *Take Your Pick*, where ordinary contestants received cash prizes, became a huge success and stayed popular for many years. It's amazing how the value of money has changed over the years – at one time £32 seemed a great deal of money! The show spawned many imitators, including *Beat the Clock,* featured on ITV's *Sunday Night at the Palladium,* which ran from 1955 until 1967. Other similar shows were *The 64,000 Dollar Question* (ITV, 1956–58), *Spot the Tune* (ITV, 1956–62), and *Criss Cross Quiz* (ITV, 1957–67). Hughie Green proved to be the perfect host for *Double Your Money* and was extremely popular with viewers.

Perhaps one of the most successful police dramas of the 1950s was *Fabian of the Yard.* It starred Bruce Seton and ran between 1954 and 1956. The show was originally transmitted on Saturday evenings but moved to Wednesday evenings and was repeated on weekday afternoons. It was shot on film unlike *Dixon of Dock Green,* which was transmitted live from the studio. The story was based on a real-life chief detective inspector. At the end of each episode, the real Bob Fabian would address the camera, although he would appear somewhat wooden after the slick performance of Bruce Seton. The series was sold to America where it was renamed *Patrol Car.*

Another popular police drama was *No Hiding Place.* It first aired on ITV in 1959 and continued until 1967. The show featured the cases of Scotland Yard's Chief Detective Superintendent Tom Lockhart (played by Raymond Francis). Johnny Briggs (who would much later play Mike Baldwin in *Coronation Street*) played DS Russell. Lockhart was one of the first television detectives to become a household name. Glyn Davies, a retired Scotland Yard officer, provided many of the storylines for the episodes. These were based on real cases. Barry Baker wrote and produced the show. By 1960, the show had an incredible audience of 7 million. *Dial 999,* first shown in 1958, was another very popular police show.

Friday Night with the Crazy Gang was broadcast on ITV in 1956. The Crazy Gang featured Bud Flanagan, Jimmy

Nervo, Teddy Knox, Charlie Naughton and Jimmy Gold. They had been incredibly popular in films during the war years and continued their act on stage to sell-out audiences under the wing of Jack Hylton. There were originally six members, but Chesney Allen retired due to ill health (amazingly he outlived them all!). The show was filmed as if it were a stage show and featured songs, a balloon dance, sketches and visual jokes. Many of the jokes were considered risqué at the time but were still included in the show. By the time the show reached the television, all of its stars were over sixty years old but were still incredibly energetic and lived up to their name well.

The Good Old Days was first broadcast in 1953 and amazingly carried on until 1983. It featured variety and music-hall acts and was originally broadcast from the Leeds City Varieties theatre. It featured both performers and audience dressed in period Edwardian clothing. Don Gemmell was the original announcer before he was replaced by Leonard Sachs. Many of the acts featured singers, and several others would have learnt their trade in the original music-hall theatres. The show would close with a rendition of 'Down at the Old Bull and Bush' with both cast members and the audience joining in.

Hancock's Half Hour was broadcast on the BBC between 1956 and 1960. It featured Tony Hancock as Anthony Aloysius Hancock, Sidney James as Sidney Balmoral James, John Le Mesurier as Lord Chief Justice William/Dr Francis Worthington, and Patricia Hayes as Mrs Cravatte. Most of the action took place at Hancock's home at 23 Railway Cuttings, East Cheam. The show was written by Ray Galton and Alan Simpson, and was produced by Duncan Wood. It was Britain's first situation comedy and influenced many comedy shows afterwards. The show had started off on the radio but was transferred to television as competition for the newly formed ITV. It was a great success, but Hancock felt he was being held back and ordered the writers to ditch Sid James. A series of one-man shows followed, which included notable episodes such as 'The Blood Donor' and 'The Radio Ham'. However, still unhappy, Hancock next sacked his writers. It was the end of a very successful team. He then decided to leave the BBC and work for ITV. His next series was very popular but was not up to the standard of the BBC shows. Still unhappy, he drank heavily and sadly committed suicide in 1968.

Oh Boy! was the first entirely pop and rock 'n' roll show, featuring top acts from the day. It first aired on ITV in 1958. Jack Good had produced the BBC's teen show *Six-Five Special*, which ran between 1957 and 1958. He wanted to make a show that featured all music and less sport and general content, but the BBC were unhappy with the idea so Good suggested an all-music show to the programmers at ITV and it was readily accepted. The first two shows ran in the Midlands region to start off with to see how well received the show was. It proved extremely popular, and the show received a regular Saturday nightspot. Top British rock 'n' roll acts, such as Marty Wilde, Cliff Richard and Billy Fury, made sure that the show was an instant success. It also attracted American stars, such as Conway Twitty, The Inkspots and Brenda Lee. Tony Hall and Jimmy Henney presented the show and Hall said at the time, 'I saw the two trial shows and thought they were the most exciting things I've ever seen on television. The lighting, the camera work was great, and I thought the music was swinging more than most of television's attempts to present jazz.' The performers were backed by Lord Rockingham's XI who themselves had a hit with 'Hoots Mon'. The show became the forerunner to all future pop-music shows.

Science fiction became very popular in the 1950s with many movies about invading alien creatures. On television, there was *The Quatermass Experiment*, which aired in

1953 on the BBC. The series consisted of six thirty-minute programmes, and featured Reginald Tate as Professor Bernard Quatermass, Isabel Dean as Judith Carroon, Duncan Lamont as Victor Carroon, Hugh Kelly as John Paterson and John Glen as Dr Gordon Briscoe. The first episode saw an experimental spacecraft return to earth. However, two of the three-man crew are missing and the third member is slowly turning into an alien creature. The BBC had found success with a previous one-off science-fiction drama called *Number Three*, which aired in 1953. *Quatermass* was hugely popular, and before the series had ended Hammer had secured the film rights. The leading man, Reginald Tate, died shortly before the next series, *Quatermass II*, and was replaced by John Robinson. *Quatermass* led the way for all future British sci-fi series.

Six-Five Special was another early pop show, and aired on the BBC between 1957 and 1958. It was presented by Pete Murray, Jo Douglas, Jim Dale and Freddie Mills, and featured a mixture of rock 'n' roll, jazz, sport and general interest items. Pete Murray opened the first show with the line 'Welcome aboard the Six-Five Special. We've got almost a hundred cats jumping here, some real cool characters to give us the gas, so just get on with it and have a ball.' This is probably how the older generation at the BBC thought that the younger generation talked all the time. The show featured the house band, 'Don Lang and his Frantic Five', who backed many of the artists who appeared on the show. They also provided the theme to the show, which featured the words 'The Six-Five Special's steaming down the line, The Six-Five Special's right on time.' This was sung over a scene of a speeding steam train.

Sunday Night at the London Palladium was first broadcast in 1955. It was made by ATV for ITV and featured Bruce Forsyth as one of its main presenters. Other compères included Tommy Trinder, Dickie Henderson, Bob

Monkhouse, Hughie Green, Alfred Marks, Robert Morley, Norman Vaughan, Jimmy Tarbuck, Jim Dale and Ted Rogers. Each show ran for an hour and it became one of the most watched programmes at the time. Created by Vic Parnell, its format consisted of a variety bill and included acts from Tiller Girls and novelty acts, including acrobats, mime artists, puppeteers etc. After the end of the first half, the mini game show *Beat the Clock* would take over before the star act finished the show. All performers would be featured on a revolving stage as the show ended. Amazingly, the same format continued until 1974. The acts originally came from music hall, but as television grew more popular many stars were drawn not only from television itself, but also from the pop world.

What's My Line? was an immensely popular television panel show that was hosted by both Eamonn Andrews and David Jacobs. It was originally broadcast by the BBC and was shown weekly until 1964 (although it was later revived). The show involved celebrity panellists trying to guess the occupation of a mystery guest. The guest would come on and mime his occupation, and the celebrities would ask questions to try and discover what they did for a living. Regular celebrity panellists included Gilbert Harding, Barbara Kelly, Lady Isobel Barnett and the magician David Nixon.

Other well-remembered shows of the 1950s included *Armchair Theatre*, *Zootime* and George Orwell's *1984*.

Armchair Theatre aired in 1956 and, like most dramas of the day, was transmitted live. This led to problems when one actor, Gareth Jones, collapsed and died during transmission. The series of programmes covered a whole range of subjects, including romance, sci-fi, comedy and thrillers as well as more high-brow drama.

Zootime was presented by Desmond Morris and was first broadcast on ITV in 1956. The show relied heavily on outside broadcasts, featuring animals from London Zoo in Regent's Park and occasionally from Whipsnade Zoo in Bedfordshire. Smaller animals, such as young chimps, were sometimes seen in the studio alongside the presenter. The show ran until 1968.

Other well-loved shows included *Blue Peter* (1958 onwards), *Crackerjack* (1955–84), *The Appleyards* (1952–57), *Before Your Very Eyes* (1956–58), *The Dickie Henderson Half Hour* (1958–59), *Emergency Ward 10* (1957–67), *Ivor the Engine* (1959–64), *Juke Box Jury* (1959–67), *Rag, Tag and Bobtail* (1953–54), *Take Your Pick* (1955–68), *Whack-O* (1956–60) and many more.

ITV also imported shows from America, such as *I Love Lucy* (1955–65) with Lucille Ball and Desi Arnaz; *Perry Mason* (1957–66) starring Raymond Burr; *Wagon Train* (1958–65) with Ward Bond; *Highway Patrol* (1956–58) starring Broderick Crawford; *77 Sunset Strip* (1958–64) starring Efrem Zimbalist Jr and Edd Byrnes; and *The Phil Silvers Show* (Bilko).

Adverts took off on the television when the ITV channel first started broadcasting in 1955. The first advert was for SR Toothpaste and aired at 8.12 p.m. on 22 September 1955 in between a variety show hosted by Jack Jackson. The advert showed a tube of toothpaste embedded in ice as a woman happily brushed her teeth. The slogan was

It's tingling fresh.
It's fresh as ice.
It's Gibbs SR toothpaste

and was voiced over by Alex Macintosh, who announced programmes on the BBC and also hosted *Come Dancing* as a regional presenter. The product chosen to be used as the first advert was selected randomly from a list of adverts put forward, which included ones for Brown & Poulson

Custard, Guinness, National Benzole, Summer County Margarine and Surf.

The first advert for Murray Mints was also shown in 1955 and included the slogan 'Murray Mints, the too-good-to-hurry-mints'. The jingle featured the voices of the Stargazers who went on to back Cliff Adams on *Sunday Night at the London Palladium* three months later. They announced that they were going to finish the set with their latest recording. Complete with bearskin hats, they re-enacted the advert as it was on the television, before throwing packets of Murray Mints into the audience. The crowd laughed, cheered and applauded loudly. The power of the television advert had arrived.

In 1956, Rowntrees came up with the slogan 'Don't forget the Fruit Gums, Mum!' and a television advert soon followed. This led to children repeating the phrase in streets and playgrounds up and down the land. Amazingly, the advertising authorities thought that the phrase put unfair pressure on mums, so the slogan was changed to 'Don't forget the Fruit Gums, Chum!' However, by then, the original slogan was set in children's minds and continued to be shouted at every opportunity.

Cigarettes were widely advertised and one television advert showed a Frank Sinatra lookalike (played by actor Terence Brooks). He was shown wearing a trench coat and standing on a London street lighting up a cigarette. The accompanying slogan stated, 'You're never alone with a Strand.' The theme tune to the advert was so popular that, as soon as it was shown, people phoned in to see if it was available on record. Cliff Adams, who'd written the jingle, quickly made a record, which was called 'The Lonely Man Theme'. It was sent out to shopkeepers in promotional cardboard packaging. The B-side featured Jimmy Lloyd singing 'You're never alone with a Strand.' Other cigarette slogans of the time included 'Never go without a Capstan.'

Most children of the time would have been used to their mothers and fathers smoking without a second thought being given to it.

Tony Solomon was a chief advertising executive and was promoting Esso Blue Paraffin. The voice-over actor didn't turn up so Solomon said that he would give it a go. He jokingly said, 'I'm your Esso Blee Dooler' instead of 'I'm your Esso Blue Dealer'. It raised such a laugh at the recording that the phrase 'Esso Blee Dooler' was featured in future adverts. The advert featured a cartoon showing a character called Joe, who was a salesman for Esso Blue Paraffin but found himself often tongue-tied. Paraffin was commonly used in households in the 1950s.

Television adverts had suddenly taken off in a big way and were guaranteed to ensure that a product and slogan were well-known. Other adverts included Tony Hancock telling everyone to 'go to work on an egg' and soap adverts with slogans such as 'Cadum for Madam'.

The Daz White Knights adverts featured knights travelling up and down the country giving away £5 and £10 prizes to housewives who washed their clothes in Daz and had a box ready to show the caller. This led to housewives buying the product more just in case one of the White Knights knocked on the door. In the 1950s, a prize of £5 or £10 was a lot of money and no one wanted to miss out.

Petrol companies also advertised on the television with the slogans 'Go well, go Shell' and 'The Esso sign means happy motoring.'

Sooty promoted Oxo to begin with, but this was followed by series of adverts featuring 'Katie', a mother and housewife played by actress Mary Holland.

Other brands that became extremely popular because of television included Mother's Pride, Carnation Milk, Ribena, Lyril soap, Phensic (with the slogan 'better for headaches than Aspirin alone'), Horlicks, Polo ('the mint with the hole'), Hovis ('don't say brown say Hovis'), Mackeson ('looks good, tastes good and by golly, it does you good'), Fry's Turkish Delight ('full of Eastern promise') and Tide washing powder (whose slogan was 'gets clothes the cleanest').

One of the most popular adverts featured the PG Tips chimps. The adverts using the chimps began in 1956 and featured the voices of popular celebrities of the day including Peter Sellers and Bob Monkhouse.

Other adverts were aimed at children and included Rice Krispies with the slogan 'Snap, Crackle and Pop', which had kids leaning over their cereal to see if they could hear the same noises.

It's amazing that at the beginning of the decade hardly anyone had a television set, but, because of the coronation, by the end of the decade most people owned one and there was a vast array of programmes to watch.

The Cinema

A trip to the cinema in the 1950s was a regular event and there were many picture houses to choose from. Queues regularly formed around the building when the main cinema was showing the latest blockbuster. There's no doubt that not only did the 1950s have some of the best films ever made but also some of the biggest stars, including John Wayne, Alan Ladd, Gary Cooper, Frank Sinatra, Burt Lancaster, Tony Curtis, Frank Sinatra, Paul Newman and Gregory Peck. There were plenty of popular British stars too, such as Alec Guinness, Richard Todd, Michael Redgrave, Peter Cushing, Christopher Lee and Jack Hawkins. It was certainly a golden age for films.

Trips to the cinema were popular and included a Pathé newsreel, cartoons and a double bill. Saturday-morning children's cinema clubs would show serials and main films, including *Flash Gordon, Tom Mix, Hopalong Cassidy, The Three Stooges* and *Popeye*.

The Second World War was still fresh in people's minds and there were many British films made about it during the 1950s. The on-screen action stoked the imaginations of boys in the 1950s and they re-enacted scenes on the streets and many bomb sites that still existed.

Dambusters starred Richard Todd as Wing Commander Guy Gibson and told the true story of Dr Barnes Wallis and his invention, the bouncing bomb, which was used to destroy the Ruhr dams. Directed by Michael Anderson, the film also starred Michael Redgrave as Dr Barnes N. Wallis, Derek Farr as Group Captain J. N. H. Whitworth, Ursula Jeans as Mrs Wallis and Basil Sydney as Air Chief Marshal Sir Arthur Harris.

Another memorable movie was *Bridge over the River Kwai*, which was released in 1957 and directed by David Lean. It had an array of famous stars appearing in it, including William Holden, Alec Guinness and Jack Hawkins. It told the story of the British soldiers held in a Japanese prisoner of war camp who were ordered to construct a bridge across the Kwai River.

Ice Cold in Alex was released in 1958 and featured John Mills as Captain Anson, Sylvia Syms as Sister Diana Murdoch, Anthony Quayle as Captain Van Der Poel, Harry Andrews as M. S. M. Tom Pugh and Diane Clare as Sister Denise Norton. It told the story of two British officers assigned to accompany an ambulance to Alexandria, and the scrapes they encounter along the way. It was one of the first British war films to feature a German sympathetically.

British comedies were popular in the 1950s and it was also the decade when the first Carry On films were made. The first was *Carry On Sergeant*, released in 1958, which saw a retired sergeant (played by William Hartnell) leading a squad of National Service conscripts through their basic training with often hilarious results. The cast included Bob Monkhouse as Charlie Sage, Shirley Eaton as Mary Sage, Eric Barker as Captain Potts and Dora Bryan as a NAAFI girl, Nora. The film cashed in on the popularity of the hit ITV show *The Army Game*. The television show had already spawned a spin-off movie called *I Only Arsked!* which featured Bernard Bresslaw, Michael Medwin, Alfie Bass, Charles Hawtrey and Michael Bentine. The film was made on a budget of £74,000 and the actors were paid a few hundred pounds each. It was a huge success and was followed later in 1959 by *Carry On Nurse*, which starred Kenneth Connor, Shirley Eaton, Hattie Jacques, Leslie Phillips, Joan Sims, Kenneth Williams, Wilfrid Hyde White, Charles Hawtrey and Joan Hickson. Most went on to appear in many of the subsequent Carry On films. *Carry On Nurse* featured the many comic mishaps that occurred on the men's ward of Haven Hospital. The success of *Carry On Sergeant* encouraged the director and screenwriter to come up with a similar film, which proved even more successful than the first. Many of the actors that appeared in the original film also appeared in the second.

Another genre of British film that appeared in the 1950s was the horror film and the most popular were made by Hammer. *The Curse of Frankenstein*, released in 1957, starred Peter Cushing as Baron Victor Frankenstein and Christopher Lee as the creature. It soon made stars of them both. The director, Terence Fisher, had to rethink the story of Frankenstein and had to make the monster unlike the one that appeared in Universal's successful films, starring Boris Karloff, of the 1930s and 1940s. The monster had to be seen as different, as Universal were very protective of the image of Frankenstein that they had created, complete with flat head and electrodes sticking out of its neck. Make-up artist Phil Leakey drew inspiration from Mary Shelley's original novel and created a creature completely different to the one featured in earlier films. It was the stuff of nightmares and any young boy who managed to see it in the 1950s probably had many sleepless nights.

Christopher Lee and Peter Cushing appeared together again in *Dracula*, which was released in 1958. Cushing played Dr Van Helsing and Christopher Lee played the memorable title role, again leading to nightmares and sleepless nights for many boys. Terence Fisher again directed this Hammer movie, fresh from the success of *The Curse of Frankenstein* the previous year. The film remains highly memorable to anyone who has ever seen it – Christopher Lee plays the part of Dracula menacingly and gives an unforgettable performance.

Hammer once more reunited the team of director Terence Fisher and actors Peter Cushing and Christopher Lee in 1959 in *The Hound of the Baskervilles*. Peter Cushing played Sherlock Holmes, Christopher Lee played Sir Henry Baskerville and André Morell played Dr Watson. Holmes and Watson are enlisted by Baskerville to track down a huge mysterious hound that roams Dartmoor. It became the first Sherlock Holmes film to be made in colour, and once more proved a huge success for Hammer.

Many titles at the time would have been X-rated, meaning that they were for adults only, but many enterprising kids managed to somehow sneak in and see the films. A commissionaire was always on the lookout for any misbehaviour, especially during the showings of films that children were allowed to see. Any disturbance and they would be turfed out of the cinema.

Ealing comedies were well established by the 1950s. *The Lavender Hill Mob* starred Alec Guinness as Henry Holland, Stanley Holloway as Alfred Pendlebury, Sidney James as 'Lackery' Wood, Alfie Bass as 'Shorty' and Marjorie Fielding as Mrs Chalk. The film was released in 1951 and told the story of a mild-mannered bank clerk who decides to steal a consignment of gold bullion and enlists the help of local businessmen. It was directed by Charles Crichton and written by T. E. B. Clarke; both were responsible for the earlier successful films *Hue and Cry* (1947) and *The Titfield Thunderbolt* (1953). *The Lavender Hill Mob* was a likeable film with engaging, eccentric characters and was a huge hit with filmgoers.

Ealing's other comedies made in the 1950s included *The Magnet* (1950), *The Man in the White Suit* (1951), *The*

Titfield Thunderbolt (1953), *The Maggie* (1954) and *The Ladykillers* (1955).

The Man in the White Suit (1951) featured Ealing regular Alec Guinness. It tells the story of a young inventor who discovers a material that is not only indestructible but also repels dirt. However, he soon finds himself in trouble not just with the textile industries but also with the workers and trade unions, who soon realise that the invention will put them out of work. The climax of the film shows Guinness as Sidney Stratton pursued by an angry mob. As he is cornered, the suit begins to fall apart as the chemical structure of the fibre breaks down. The crowd tear bits of it off until Stratton is left in just his underwear. The film also starred Joan Greenwood as Daphne Birnley, Cecil Parker as Alan Birnley and Michael Gough as Michael Corland.

The Titfield Thunderbolt (1953) told the story of a group of villagers who decide to run their own train service when the branch line is threatened with closure. It starred Stanley Holloway as Mr Valentine, George Relph as Vicar Samuel Weech, Naunton Wayne as Mr Blakeworth, John Gregson as Gordon Chesterworth and Godfrey Tearle as Bishop Olly Matthews. The film was the first Ealing comedy to be shot in colour and, although well known, was only a moderate success at the time. It shows an England now long gone, and hasn't aged as well as some of Ealing's other comedies from the time.

The Ladykillers (1955) was probably the most successful of Ealing's comedies. It starred Alec Guinness as Professor Marcus, Cecil Parker as Major Courtney, Herbert Lom as Louis Harvey, Peter Sellers as Harry Robinson, Danny Green as One-Round Lawson and Katie Johnson as Mrs Louisa Wilberforce. The story revolved around a gang of thieves who pose as a string quintet while renting lodgings from an old lady. They carry out a robbery but are ultimately defeated by the old lady and turn on one another. The idea for the film came to the writer, William Rose, in a dream. He had also written Ealing's previous film, *The Maggie*, the story of a captain of an old boat who tricks American businessmen into letting them carry his cargo. *The Maggie* is a film largely forgotten when people think about Ealing comedies. *The Ladykillers* was the last of the big comedies from Ealing. Two more minor films followed before the studio closed. The film was a huge success both in Britain and America. It also featured Herbert Lom in his first comic role.

Earlier, in February 1950, Ealing Studios had also released *The Blue Lamp*, which starred Jack Warner as Dixon of Dock Green. He was killed in the film but was later resurrected for a long-running television series.

Perhaps children looked more towards American films than British ones for entertainment. Everything about America seemed exciting and more appealing. Westerns and war films were incredibly popular.

Films such as *The Story of Robin Hood and His Merrie Men*, *The Seventh Voyage of Sinbad*, and *Ben-Hur* (1959) all fired up a young boy's imagination. Many films would have had children playing in the streets straight afterwards, pretending to be Romans, outlaws or pirates.

Science fiction also played a huge part in cinema in the 1950s, with films like *When Worlds Collide* (1951) starring Richard Derr; *20,000 Leagues Under the Sea* (1954), a Walt Disney film starring Kirk Douglas and James Mason; *The Day the Earth Stood Still* (1951) starring Michael Rennie; *The Thing from Another World* (1951) featuring James Arness; *The War of the Worlds* (1953) starring Gene Barry, *It Came from Outer Space* (1953), filmed in 3D and starring Richard Carlson; *Creature from the Black Lagoon* (1954) again featuring Richard Carlson; *Them!* (1954) starring James Whitmore; *This Island Earth* (1955) with Jeff Morrow; *Godzilla* (1954) starring Akira

Takarada; *Earth* vs *the Flying Saucers* (1956) featuring Hugh Marlowe; *Invasion of the Body Snatchers* (1956) starring Kevin McCarthy and Dana Wynter; *The Incredible Shrinking Man* (1957) with Grant Williams; *The Fly* (1958) starring David Hedison; and *The Forbidden Planet* (1956) with Walter Pidgeon and Leslie Nielsen.

Audiences were in for a treat when they visited the cinema, with new effects such as 3D. *Creature from the Black Lagoon* was shot and originally released in 3D which required cinemagoers to wear special polarised 3D glasses.

All these films had young boys looking skyward during the day for spaceships, and under their beds at night-time for aliens or monsters!

Boys loved Westerns and there were many of them to see at the local picture house. James Stewart starred in *Winchester '73* (1950), John Wayne starred in *The Searchers* (1956), and Alan Ladd starred in *The Badlanders* (1958). Other Westerns included *Broken Arrow* (1950) with James Stewart and Jeff Chandler; *The Big Country* (1958) starring Gregory Peck, Jean Simmons, Burl Ives and Charlton Heston; *The Fiend Who Walked the West* (1958) starring Robert Walker; *Gunfight at the O. K. Coral* (1957) starring Kirk Douglas and Burt Lancaster; *High Noon* (1952) starring Gary Cooper and Grace Kelly; *The Left Handed Gun* (1958) starring Paul Newman; *The Man from Laramie* (1955) starring James Stewart; *Rio Bravo* (1959) starring John Wayne, Dean Martin and Ricky Nelson; *Rio Grand* (1950) starring John Wayne; *Shane* (1953) with Alan Ladd; and *The Bravados* (1958) starring Gregory Peck and Joan Collins.

Abbott and Costello were hugely popular and starred in several movies in the 1950s, including *Abbott and Costello in the Foreign Legion* (1950), *Abbott and Costello Meet the Invisible Man* (1951), *Abbott and Costello Go to*

Mars (1953) and *Abbott and Costello Meet the Mummy* (1955).

Adventure films included *The Adventures of Robinson Crusoe* (1954) starring Daniel O'Herlihy; *Around the World in 80 Days* (1956) with David Niven, Cantinflas, Robert Newton and Shirley MacLaine; *Ben-Hur* (1959) with Charlton Heston; *The Buccaneer* (1958) starring Yul Brynner, Charles Boyer and Charlton Heston; *The Crimson Pirate* (1952) with Burt Lancaster, Nick Cravat and Eva Bartok; *Journey to the Centre of the Earth* (1959) with Pat Boone and James Mason; and *Tarzan's Greatest Adventure* (1959) starring Gordon Scott (as Tarzan) together with Sean Connery and Anthony Quayle. *Davy Crockett: King of the Wild Frontier* (1955), starring Fess Parker and Buddy Ebsen, was a compilation of three episodes of Walt Disney's extremely popular television show. The show was very popular with boys, who all wanted a Davy Crockett-type hat. Disney's merchandising machine meant that they soon became available and incredibly sold in their thousands. For a while, every young boy wanted to be Davy Crockett. The 1950s was really the first decade that showed what an influence the power of film and television had on it viewers, and the money that could be made from merchandise. Disney tried to create other similar successful characters such as *The Saga of Andy Burnett* (1957) and *Texas John Slaughter* (1958) but none had the appeal of Davy Crockett.

War films included *The Battle of the River Plate* (1959), *Dunkirk* (1958), *Flying Leathernecks* (1951) starring John Wayne and Robert Ryan, and *The Dam Busters* (1954).

There were also movies featuring the latest rock 'n' roll stars, such as Elvis Presley in *Love Me Tender* (1956), *Loving You* (1957), *Jailhouse Rock* (1957) and *King Creole* (1958), and Cliff Richard in *Expresso Bongo* (1959).

Other musicals included *Gigi* (1958); *Guys and Dolls*; *High Society* (1956) starring Frank Sinatra, Bing Crosby and

Grace Kelly; *The King and I* (1956) starring Yul Brynner; *Oklahoma!* (1955); *Seven Brides for Seven Brothers* (1954); *Singin' in the Rain* (1952) with Gene Kelly; *South Pacific* (1958); *An American in Paris* (1951) with Gene Kelly and Leslie Caron; *Annie Get Your Gun* (1950); *Carmen Jones* (1954); and *Carousel* (1956).

Alfred Hitchcock films included *North by Northwest* (1959) starring Cary Grant, Eva Marie Saint and James Mason; *Rear Window* (1954) starring James Stewart and Grace Kelly; *Strangers on a Train* (1951) with Robert Walker; *To Catch a Thief* (1955) with Cary Grant; and *Dial M for Murder* (1954) starring Ray Milland and Grace Kelly.

Children's films included *Treasure Island* (1950); Walt Disney's *Alice in Wonderland* (1951); *Hans Christian Andersen* (1952) starring Danny Kaye; *Peter Pan* (1953); *Lady and the Tramp* (1955); *The Shaggy Dog* (1959) starring Fred MacMurray; *Sleeping Beauty* (1959); and *Cinderella* (1950).

Classic films of the decade included *Giant* (1956) starring James Dean, Rock Hudson and Elizabeth Taylor; *Harvey* with James Stewart; *Ice Cold in Alex* (1958); *The Night of the Hunter* (1955) starring Robert Mitchum; *On the Waterfront* (1954) starring Marlon Brando; *Rebel Without a Cause* (1955) starring James Dean; *The Seven Year Itch* (1955); *Some Like It Hot* (1959) with Jack Lemmon, Tony Curtis and Marilyn Monroe; *A Streetcar Named Desire* (1951); *The Ten Commandments* (1956) with Charlton Heston; *The Wild One* (1953) with Marlon Brando; *The African Queen* (1951) with Humphrey Bogart and Katherine Hepburn; *Ben-Hur* (1959) starring Charlton Heston; *Cat on a Hot Tin Roof* (1958); *The Defiant Ones* (1958) starring Tony Curtis and Sidney Poitier; *East of Eden* (1955) starring James Dean, Julie Harris and Raymond Massey; *From Here to Eternity* (1953) starring Burt Lancaster, Montgomery

Clift and Frank Sinatra; and *Gentlemen Prefer Blondes* (1953).

A trip to the cinema in the 1950s included queuing around the building to see the latest blockbuster. Any nonsense, naughty behaviour or cheek from children could mean that the commissionaire refused them entry or threw them out for misbehaving during the film. Jumping over seats during an action movie was common practice, as was throwing things at your friends, especially during children's performances. Most of the time, it didn't matter if you were thrown out (as long as your parents didn't find out!), as there would be another cinema just down the road. Of course it would be showing a different film and you were only safe if the commissionaire hadn't phoned ahead to the next cinema to let them know you were coming!

Tales of pirates, adventurers, Tarzan, Robin Hood, cowboys, soldiers, monsters and even Abbott and Costello all had boys re-enacting scenes the next day in the playground, woods or the nearest bomb site.

Food and Household Shopping

Much of the food within a household was bought daily at the nearby grocer's. Children were regularly sent on errands for essentials and got to know the shopkeeper well. Many items would be bought 'on account' and the bill paid at the end of the week. Houses had a simple pantry where food was kept fresh for as long as possible.

Milk was delivered by a man on a horse and cart (there were far more horse-driven vehicles in the 1950s). Milk would be kept in its bottle in a bucket of cold water to keep it from going off. Boiling it would also make it last a bit longer.

The baker's van would deliver straight to the door, not only bringing freshly baked bread but also treats for the children like Wagon Wheels, which were a lot bigger then than they are today!

Popular breakfast cereals for children included Corn Flakes, Cubs, Sugar Puffs, Energen Breakfast Flakes, Shreddies, Force Wheat Flakes, Grape-Nuts, Kellogg's Sugar Frosted Flakes (Frosties), Quaker Puffed Wheat, Kellogg's All Bran, Kellogg's Rice Crispies, Kellogg's Bran Flakes and Scott's Oats.

The advert for Weetabix showed a little girl in spotted pyjamas and read 'Have you bringed my Weetabix breakfast? ... cos when I'm dressed I'll want my breakfast. Mummy says Weetabix is ever so good 'n keeps me warm like 'Golly's' coat, only Weetabix is inside. An' after breakfast I'll go and play … I can play and play all day an' never stop.'

The advert continued 'Clever Mummy! She knows that Weetabix is the best way of giving her children the energy they need. Made with whole wheat, which includes the natural Germ of the Wheat with its health-giving properties, Weetabix is packed with warmth-giving energy.'

The local grocer would slice bacon in front of you, cut cheese from a large block with a wire and stock exotic items like prunes in open sacks on the floor. The grocer always fetched what the customer required and there was no self-service. The shopkeeper would get to know all his customers by name and some would hang around and chat; some grocers would even get out a chair for them!

Larger shops like the Co-op, Woolworths and Lipton's existed, and a variety of items including broken biscuits could be bought there.

For the children, the Corona man would come to the house delivering pop in glass bottles. Many kids made sure they saved the 'empties' as they could redeem 2*d* on them when they gave them back. Some kids even went searching for them so they could make extra money. This practice went on well into the 1970s.

The Festival of Britain in 1951 showed the British public a whole new range of products, including sleek fitted kitchens, furniture and appliances. With the advent of the refrigerator, it became possible to store food for much longer. Birds Eye fish fingers were first produced in 1955. However, with only 8 per cent of households owning a fridge in the mid-1950s, many children didn't get the chance to eat them until much later.

Suddenly a whole variety of new products appeared on the shelves. A typical shopping basket would contain all the usual items, such as meat, potatoes, carrots, etc., as well as many new items. For people with fridges, there were Birds Eye frozen peas and fish fingers. To go with a meal, there was HP sauce, Daddies sauce and SAXA salt.

Margarines had become more popular than butter and included Stork margarine, Echo margarine or Kraft margarine. Popular beverages included Maxwell House coffee, Nescafé instant coffee, Lyons instant coffee, Camp coffee, Cadbury's Bournville, Typhoo Tea, Lyons Tea, Brooke Bond, Lyons tea, Fry's Cocoa, Nesquik and Cadbury's drinking chocolate at 1s 9d a half-pound.

The advert for Nestlé's Nescafé (pronounced then as 'Nes-cafee' not 'Nes-cafay') pure instant coffee showed a posh woman sitting on a chaise longue sipping from a china cup. It read,

> Here's coffee that's worth sipping slowly, enjoying the roaster-fresh smell, the full round flavour. And every cup is fresh and perfect, for with Nescafé there's no delay, nothing to go wrong in the making. You really must try Nescafé, and when you do, you'll find that Nescafé gives you the most economical way of enjoying really good coffee whenever you want it.

Varieties of pop for the kids included, as mentioned, Corona, Tizer and Lucozade, although Lucozade was seen more as a 'pick you up drink' when you were ill. Lucozade's advert showed a smiling young woman in bed being given Lucozade by a nurse, with the caption 'she'll soon be up and about again!' The advert said that it was used by doctors and nurses in hospitals as well as by clinics and schools. Kia-ora was also available. For a treat there were Cadbury's Milk Fingers, Smith's Crisps, Cadbury's Chocolate Sandwich and Orange Sandwich both at 2s a half-pound. There was also Bird's custard powder for 'cream-smooth' custard to put on puddings, etc.; a box cost 10d.

Washing powders included Persil ('washes whiter'), Fab, Omo, Tide, Surf and Lux while household cleaners included Flash, Harpic, Pledge, Domestos, Ajax and Brillo soap pads (twelve for 2*s* 3*d*), Bronco antiseptic toilet tissue which came as shiny crisp paper in a box, or the deluxe paper version which came on a roll.

Meals could be prepared on one of the new modern cookers available such as the Cannon, complete with foldaway eye-level grill. The advert stated that it grilled '8 chops, 2½ lb sirloin, 2 small chickens, 4 large fish fillets, 4 large steaks, 4 pigeons and 1½ lbs of sausages and dozens of other dishes never before possible on an ordinary cooker!' The advert boasted that it contained 'a marvellous oven – it takes a 22 lb turkey, a 4-burner hotplate with automatic lighting and a warming draw for plates and dishes. Available on extended terms for a small deposit. Visit your local gas showroom today!'

The Main Century was a similar popular cooker that came in several colours, including cream, cream and green and cream and blue. A Main gas cookery book was also available for 5*s* 6*d*, which showed you all the things you could make with your new cooker.

It all seems commonplace today, but a cooker like this, back in the 1950s, would have been state-of-the-art technology.

Speaking in 1957, the Prime Minister Harold Macmillan gave a speech saying, 'most of our people have never had it so good'. Over the years, this quote has been paraphrased and become 'Britain has never had it so good', which, in many ways, it hadn't. For many people, things were definitely on the up.

12

Comics and Books

The comics that children loved to read in the 1950s included *The Beano*, *The Dandy*, *Eagle*, *Buster*, *The Rover*, *The Hotspur*, *The Topper*, *The Beezer* and *Girl*. American comics were also very popular with boys. Much-loved books included *Treasure Island*, *Peter Pan*, *Wind in the Willows*, *The Lion, the Witch and the Wardrobe* and *Winnie the Pooh*.

The Dandy first came out in 1937 and *The Beano* followed it in 1938. They were published on alternate weeks during the Second World War because of paper and ink rationing. By 1949, normal weekly publishing continued, and during the 1950s the comics were well read by boys all over the country. Popular characters in *The Beano* included Biffo the Bear, Roger the Dodger, Minnie the Minx, The Bash Street Kids and Lord Snooty. Dennis the Menace first appeared in issue 452 on 17 March 1951 and became the comic's longest-running strip.

Popular characters in *The Dandy* included Korky the Cat and Desperate Dan, which have become the comic's longest-running strips. The first issue of *The Dandy* was published on 4 December 1937. It was then known as *The Dandy Comic*. It was different from other comics of the day because it used speech balloons instead of captions. The comic was well established by the 1950s and on 17 July 1950 its name was changed from *The Dandy Comic* to just *The Dandy*. The first *Dandy* annual was released in 1938. It was originally called *The Dandy Monster Comic*. The annual has been published every year ever since. The annuals always came out at Christmas time, and boys in the 1950s all loved getting a copy of *The Dandy* or *The Beano* as a Christmas present. In 1954, the first Desperate Dan book was published. It mostly consisted of strips that had appeared in the comic throughout the year. *The Dandy* eventually consisted of all comic strips, but the earlier issues had also included text strips with only some illustrations. Some of these text strips included Jimmy's Pocket Grandpa, British Boys and Girls Go West, There's a Curse on the King and Swallowed by a Whale.

The Beano's first edition appeared on 30 July 1938 and became D. C. Thomson & Co.'s most popular comic. The name *Beano* came from an English word which means 'good time'. Boys in the 1950s didn't think to keep their old comics and they were swapped in the playground. Today, there are only twelve known copies of the first issue *Beano* and one recently sold for over £12,000. A first issue of *The Dandy* fetched over £20,000 at auction.

Like *The Dandy*, *The Beano* released a yearly annual, which was first published in 1939. Throughout the 1950s, the annual featured Biffo the Bear on the cover. Until 1957, it cost 6*s* and then cost 6*s* 6*d* until 1960. *The Beano Book* of 1953 contained comic strips of Biffo the Bear, Lord Snooty, Pansy Potter, Postie Hastie, Dennis the Menace, Sinbad the Sailor, Hawk-Eye Bravest of the Braves, Have-a-go Joe, Maxy's Taxi and many more. There were also text stories which included 'The Clockwork Cop', 'The Bird Boy', 'Ginger's Magic Ear' and 'Waltzing Matilda'.

Other comics available at the time included *The Beezer*, which was first published on 21 January 1956 and was of tabloid size – twice as big as other comics available at the time. Popular strips featured in the comic during the 1950s included Ginger, Bushwhacker, Mick on the Moon, Lone Wolfe, Calamity Jane, Nosey Parker, Big Ed, Smart Alice and the Banana Bunch. The Banana Bunch featured a group of kids called Brainy, Dopey, Lanky, Titch and Fatty and featured their weekly antics. A very popular strip was Colonel Blink 'the short-sighted gink', which featured a character similar to Mr Magoo with equally madcap misfortunes due to his short sight. The strip was drawn by Tom Bannister. *The Beezer*'s sister comic was *The Topper*, which first appeared on 7 February 1953. The first front cover featured a strip showing the antics of 'Mickey the Monkey'.

On 14 April 1950, the *Eagle* comic first appeared. Within its pages were strips featuring Captain Pugwash and Dan Dare. It was the idea of Marcus Morris who was an Anglican vicar from Lancashire. Previously, Morris had edited a parish church magazine called the *Anvil*, which was illustrated by Frank Hampson. Morris felt that the *Anvil* wasn't communicating the word of the Church to a large audience, so with Hampson he created a mock-up comic book featuring Christian values. The idea was offered to several Fleet Street publishers but little interest was shown in it. However, eventually the Hulton Press took on the idea and the *Eagle* was born. A huge publicity campaign ensured that the first issued sold over 900,000 copies. The front page featured, in full colour, 'Dan Dare, Pilot of the Future'. The cover was drawn by Hampson. Other characters appearing in the comic included Riders of the Range and PC 49. There were also news and sport sections together with cutaway drawings of complicated machinery. Readers could join a club which offered all sorts of merchandise for sale including toothpaste, pyjamas, and toy ray guns. There were several disputes when the comic was taken over by a new publisher, and Morris left in 1959 with Hampson leaving soon after.

Girl was a comic aimed solely at girls. There were many comics for boys, particularly *Eagle*, on the market and it was felt that a similar comic should be produced for girls. The first copy appeared on 2 November 1951 and featured 'Kitty Hawke and her All-Girl Air Crew'. The comic was a sister paper to the *Eagle* and was again produced by the Hulton Press with most of its pages in full colour. The idea was once more that of the Reverend Marcus Morris and the main story was illustrated by Ray Bailey. The Kitty Hawke strip proved not to be very popular and was thought to be too masculine. It featured the exploits of a group of women who ran a chartered airline. Perhaps it was too much like Dan Dare. Eventually, the strip was moved inside the comic to its black and white pages and Wendy and Jinx was moved to the front cover. Wendy and Jinx told the story of two girls at Manor School and stayed on the cover until 1958. Other stories within the comic included Angela Air Hostess, At Work with Janet – Fashion Artist, Belle of the Ballet, Emergency Ward 10 (based on the popular television series), Lindy Love, and Susan of St Brides. The first issue cost 4½d. The comic continued throughout the 1950s and was eventually merged with *Princess* in 1964. Most comics produced a yearly annual, which would appear just in time for the Christmas market.

American comics were hugely popular. At the beginning of the 1950s, crime and horror comics reached Britain, arriving on ships from America. These included titles like *Tales from the Crypt* and *The Vault of Horror*. At first, they were only available in cities with ports, such as Liverpool, Manchester, London and Belfast. However, using matrices imported from America, the comics were soon printed in

London and Leicester and sold in backstreet newsagents. There was a moral panic over the American comics, which were seen unfit for British children of the time. Questions were raised in parliament. Several prominent people, including the Most Reverend Geoffrey Fisher, the Archbishop of Canterbury, Major Gwilym Lloyd George, the Home Secretary and Minister of Welsh Affairs, and the National Union of Teachers. This led to the Children and Young Persons (Harmful Publications) Act of 1955 banning children from obtaining publications of a horrific or repulsive nature. The Act is still in place today although many boys of the 1950s, and many since, have read comics like *Tales from the Crypt* or *The Vault of Horror*. Other comics produced in Britain at the time which were shunned by the establishment included titles such as *Spellbound*, *Suspense*, *Spaceman*, *Out of the World*, *Race for the Moon*, *The Human Torch*, and *Adventures into the Unknown*, etc. All were popular but short-lived because of the Act.

American comics featured something every boy was interested in: superheroes. The comics were hard to obtain but popular ones featured Superman, Batman, Captain America, Wonder Woman and Captain Marvel.

Other titles covered mystery and science fiction, such as *Astonishing*, *Amazing Mysteries*, *Strange Tales*, *Journey into Mystery*, *Menace*, and *Journey into Unknown Worlds*, etc.

If your father worked in the docks or abroad then the titles were far easier to obtain.

The *Boy's Own* paper was a monthly booklet that featured articles on football, building balsa-wood aeroplanes, locomotives, sledging, boxing, cricket, cycling and fishing as well as exciting stories of Red Indians, pirates and wartime adventures. Each magazine cost 1 shilling and promoted outdoor activities and hobbies, as well as including educational articles.

I-Spy books proved very popular, especially with boys. The idea came from an article in the *News Chronicle*, in which, every day, an article appeared written by 'Big Chief I-Spy' (Head of the Redskins). The article recorded his I-Spy triumphs in tracking and spotting. Every day there were messages and passwords printed for members of the club who were known as the Great Tribe. Booklets could be bought for 6*d* and covered subjects such as I-Spy insects, wild fruits, fungi, wild flowers, history, the unusual, dogs, trees, and on the road, etc. The books contained many illustrations and the I-Spyer had to spot the objects and write down when and where the object was spotted. For each one seen, points were awarded. When the book was full, it could be sent to Big Chief I-Spy and an Order of Merit would be sent back together with the booklet. The books had to be signed by a teacher or parents, along with the name of the entrant's school. The craze proved incredibly popular and it continues today, although perhaps it's not quite the same. Charles Warrell produced the first I-Spy booklet in 1948, and by 1956 Arnold Cawthrow had become the second Big Chief I-Spy.

Children could enrol in the 'Great Tribe of Redskins' by buying a membership pack from their local newsagent, which included a badge and everything needed to decipher the secret messages featured each day in the *News Chronicle*. Eventually, there were endless books covering all sorts of outdoors subjects and children were encouraged to explore their environment while learning about the names of trees, flowers, insects, birds and wildlife.

Popular fiction for children during the 1950s included *The Lion, the Witch and the Wardrobe*, which was published in 1950 and written by C. S. Lewis. Geoffrey Bles, who published the book, feared that tales of fantasy might not be well received, but children loved it and soon afterwards several other works in the Narnia saga were published, including *Prince Caspian: The Return to Narnia* (1951), *The Voyage of the Dawn Treader* (1952), *The Silver Chair* (1953), *The Horse and His Boy* (1954), *The Magician's Nephew* (1955) and *The Last Battle* (1956).

Although the first in the series of Biggles books (*The Camels Are Coming*) was published in 1932, the books proved to be immensely popular with boys during the 1950s, probably because it wasn't long after the end of the Second World War. The books were written by William Earl Johns, under the pen name Captain W. E. Johns; Johns had never actually held the rank of captain. However, he was himself a pilot during the First World War. He was captured on 16 September 1918 and remained a prisoner until the end of the war. He remained in the RAF until 1927. He wrote over 160 books, with nearly 100 of them featuring Biggles, He contributed to *Modern Boy* magazine and also wrote for *Popular Flying* magazine. He continued to write books about Biggles until his death in 1968. The character of Biggles was said to be based on Air Commander Cecil George Wigglesworth, whom Johns had known during the First World War. The series of Biggles books stoked the imaginations of children during the 1950s. Invasions of Germans and enemy attacks were still fresh in everyone's minds, and children happily re-enacted war games in streets and playing fields.

13

Music

At the beginning of the 1950s, most families had a gramophone player and a selection of 78 rpm records featuring such artists as Bing Crosby, Vera Lynn, Max Bygraves and Nat 'King' Cole.

These were mainly records that parents enjoyed when not listening to the radio.

78s were made of shellac, which produced a lot of surface noise and crackling. They were heavy and prone to shattering if dropped. When vinyl was introduced, the quality improved drastically. The 45 rpm single became popular in the late 1950s as teenagers had more money to spend.

The UK singles chart started in 1952 and was the idea of Percy Dickins, who worked for the *New Musical Express* (*NME*). He wanted to produce a chart similar to the one used in the American *Billboard* magazine. A record's popularity previous to this was measured in the amount of copies of sheet music sold for that particular song. The first *NME* chart was published on 14 November 1952 and Al Martino topped it with 'Here in My Heart'.

The first chart featured many well-known names:

1 'Here in My Heart' by Al Martino
2 'You Belong To Me' by Jo Stafford

3 'Somewhere Along The Way' by Nat 'King' Cole
4 'The Isle Of Innisfree' by Bing Crosby
5 'Feet Up' by Guy Mitchell
6 'Half As Much' by Rosemary Clooney
7 'Forget Me Not' by Vera Lynn
7 'High Noon (Do Not Forsake Me)' by Frankie Laine
8 'Blue Tango' by Ray Martin
8 'Sugarbush' by Doris Day and Frankie Laine
9 'The Homing Waltz' by Vera Lynn
10 'Auf Wiederseh'n Sweetheart' by Vera Lynn
11 'Because You're Mine' by Mario Lanza
11 'Cowpuncher's Cantata' by Max Bygraves
12 'Walkin' My Baby Back Home' by Johnnie Ray

The chart featured the top twelve but some songs tied for position. The charts consisted of mainly American acts, with only three British performers getting a look in – Max Bygraves, Vera Lynn and Ray Martin. Right at the end of the chart was Johnny Ray. With his stage act, which included him pulling at his hair, falling on the stage and crying, he soon became a teen idol, and girls would scream whenever he appeared. His stage act earned him the nicknames 'Mr Emotion', The Nabob of Sob' and the 'Prince of Wails'. He dominated the chart with his single 'Cry' which featured 'The Little White Cloud that Cried' on the B-side. The 78 rpm record went on to sell 2 million copies. By Christmas 1952, the chart had changed little:

1 'Here in my Heart' by Al Martino
2 'You Belong To Me' by Jo Stafford
3 'Comes A-Long A-Love' by Kay Starr
3 'The Isle Of Innisfree' by Bing Crosby
4 'Feet Up' by Guy Mitchell
5 'Half As Much' by Rosemary Clooney
6 'Because You're Mine' by Nat 'King' Cole

6 'Somewhere Along The Way' by Nat 'King' Cole
6 'White Christmas' by Mantovani
7 'Faith Can Move Mountains' by Johnnie Ray and
The Four Lads
8 'Silent Night, Holy Night' by Bing Crosby
8 'Takes Two To Tango' by Louis Armstrong
9 'Walkin' To Missouri' by Tony Brent
10 'Because You're Mine' by Mario Lanza
10 'Forget Me Not' by Vera Lynn
10 'Sugarbush' by Doris Day and Frankie Laine
11 'Jambalaya' by Jo Stafford
12 'High Noon (Do Not Forsake Me)' by Frankie Laine

The same artists appeared over and over in the chart, and back in 1952 it was Mantovani, not Bing Crosby, having a hit with 'White Christmas'.

1953 saw a similar mix of American stars ruling the charts, including Eddie Fisher, Perry Como, Guy Mitchell and Frankie Laine. The charts of 1954 featured artists such as Frank Sinatra with 'Three Coins in a Fountain', Johnny Ray with 'Such a Night', and Eddie Calvert with 'O Mein Papa'.

Rock 'n' roll first appeared in 1955 when Bill Haley and his Comets charted in November with 'Rock Around the Clock'. A new age of music was born, although many of the mainstream artists had hit the number one spot during the year, including Dickie Valentine, Slim Whitman, Tony Bennett, Alma Cogan and even Jimmy Young with 'The Man from Laramie' and 'Unchained Melody'.

When Bill Haley and the Comets visited Great Britain in 1957, they became the first American rock 'n' roll act to tour here. They disembarked from the *Queen Elizabeth* at Southampton and reached Waterloo station in London later that day. Their arrival attracted a crowd of thousands of fans all pushing to get nearer to them. The next day, national newspapers dubbed the event 'the Second Battle of Waterloo'.

Rock 'n' roll exploded and gave birth to such artists as Little Richard, Elvis Presley, Jerry Lee Lewis, Buddy Holly, Gene Vincent and Eddie Cochran.

In Britain, the skiffle craze grew from the influence of American music, and Lonnie Donegan had a huge hit with 'Rock Island Line' in 1955.

The rock 'n' roll scene began in Britain with the screening of the films 'Blackboard Jungle' and 'Rock Around the Clock', which both featured Bill Haley and his Comets. 'Rock Around the Clock' topped the chart in both 1955 and 1956. There was an uproar when young cinemagoers ripped up the seats so they could dance to the music in the film. This linked rock 'n' roll with delinquency, which led to this type of music being banned by television and radio stations. However, with the charting of stars such as Elvis Presley, Jerry Lee Lewis and Buddy Holly, things were set to change. Britain had its own rock 'n' roll stars, including Cliff Richard, Billy Fury, Marty Wilde, Adam Faith and Tommy Steele as well as lesser-known stars such as Johnny Gentle and Duffy Power.

Elvis Presley got to number two in the UK with both 'Hound Dog' and 'Heartbreak Hotel', but his first number one hit was 'All Shook Up' in 1957. A string of hits followed, including 'Jailhouse Rock' from the movie of 1957.

Buddy Holly became popular with British audiences in 1957 with hits such as 'That'll Be The Day' and 'Peggy Sue'.

Britain produced its first proper rock 'n' roll star when Cliff Richard and his backing group, The Drifters, went to number two with 'Move It' in 1958 (although Tommy Steele had had a hit previously with 'Rock With the Caveman' and a number one hit with 'Singing the Blues' in 1956). The popularity of Cliff Richard was mainly due to appearances on ITV's *Oh Boy* show, which aired between 1958 and 1959. This followed on from the BBC's *Six-Five Special*, which aired between 1957 and 1958.

For kids who fancied themselves as rock 'n' roll stars, adverts in newspapers and magazines offered 'Rock 'n roll gitars' (guitar was deliberately misspelt) for 24*s* 6*d*. The advert read,

> The craze of the Century. They'll crowd round you when you strum. ELVIS PRESLEY the greatest U.S.A. Rock 'n' Roll star has his name on every one. Easy to play with the simple Tutor supplied free including carrying box. All fitted with nylon strings which give the good old Rock 'n' Roll and Calypso effect. Colourful to a degree, made of strong styrene for strength. Good tone, tunes accurately. Just send 24/6, plus 2/6 post etc. No more to pay. Get initiated now. Also ELVIS PRESLEY UKETTE with self-playing apparatus incorporated, 10/11 only, post etc. 2/-.

By the end of the 1950s, the pop charts contained a totally different type of music from the one shown in 1952. The number one records from 1959 included 'It's Only Make Believe' by Conway Twitty, which topped the chart for 5 weeks at the beginning of the year. This was followed by:

Jane Morgan with 'The Day The Rains Came', which stayed at number one for a week from 23 January.

Elvis Presley with 'One Night/I Got Stung' for three weeks from 30 January.

Shirley Bassey with 'As I Love You' for four weeks on 20 February.

The Platters with 'Smoke Gets in Your Eyes' for one week from 20 March.

Russ Conway with 'Side Saddle' for four weeks from 27 March.

Buddy Holly with 'It Doesn't Matter Anymore' for three weeks from 24 April.

Elvis Presley with 'A Fool Such As I/I Need Your Love Tonight' for five weeks from 15 May.

Russ Conway with 'Roulette' for two weeks from 19 June.

Bobby Darin with 'Dream Lover' for four weeks from 3 July.

Cliff Richard and The Drifters with 'Living Doll' for six weeks from 31 July.

Craig Douglas with 'Only Sixteen' for four weeks from 11 September.

Jerry Keller with 'Here Comes Summer' for one week from 9 October.

Bobby Darin with 'Mack The Knife' for two weeks from 16 October.

Cliff Richard and The Shadows with 'Travellin' Light' for five weeks from 30 October.

Adam Faith with 'What Do You Want' for two weeks from December. This shared the number one spot with 'What Do You Want to Make Those Eyes at Me For' by Emile Ford and The Checkmates for one week beginning 18 December. However, 'What Do You Want to Make Those Eyes at Me For' stayed at number one for five weeks from 25 December.

By 1958, Elvis Presley had been drafted into military service. When Buddy Holly was killed in a plane crash on 3 February 1959, it seemed to signify the end of an era. The sound of rock 'n' roll became more mellow and clean-cut for the 1960s. Although rock 'n' roll continued, the middle to the end of the 1950s included many of its best artists.

Along with J. P. 'The Big Bopper' Richardson and Ritchie Valens, Holly died aboard a small chartered plane on its way to a spot in the Winter Dance Party, a three-week tour covering the Midwest of America.

Don McLean's single 'American Pie' from 1971 refers to the incident in the line 'The Day the Music Died'.

Eddie Cochran died in a car crash outside Bristol less than a year later.

When the new beat music came along in 1962, it signalled a decline in rock 'n' roll music appearing in the charts.

14

Holidays

Many families took their regular annual holiday to the seaside, staying in rundown bed-and-breakfast accommodation. There was much excitement from children, many of whom lived long distances away from the sea and dreamed of swimming, building sandcastles, riding donkeys and all the other fun that could be had at the seaside.

Many bed and breakfast owners wouldn't allow their guests in during the day, so families had to make their own entertainment, which was made more difficult by the unpredictable British weather. Arriving on holiday by coach or train was a much more common experience, as many people didn't own cars and were unable to drive to their destination themselves. Fairground attractions, candyfloss and rock all added to the appeal.

For people who didn't want to stay at bed and breakfasts, and wanted a holiday with regular meals, decent accommodation, entertainment and endless activities, holiday camps seemed very appealing.

Billy Butlin opened his first holiday camp at Skegness during the Easter holiday of 1936. It was a low-key affair and the accommodation was basic. There was no heating in the chalets and no hot water. Butlin guaranteed free entertainment to all of his campers, no matter what the English weather threw at them. As well as their accommodation, they had access to bars, dining halls and theatres. To keep out the cold, campers ate their breakfast dressed in warm clothes, and danced in their overcoats. As the first campers arrived, the camp was still incomplete and didn't have its own water supply. Water was discovered three weeks later after many boreholes had been sunk on site. Previous to the camp opening, Butlin had taken out a half-page advert in the *Daily Express* offering accommodation, four meals a day and free entertainment. He was soon inundated with enquiries, and 500 campers were expected on the day of its opening. The first campers played table tennis while the building of the camp continued around them. Even with its teething problems, over half of the people who stayed the first week booked to stay again. The popularity of the camp led to another being built at Clacton in 1938, and the construction of a third camp at Filey began in 1939.

When the Second World War broke out, completion of the Filey camp was postponed and both the camps at Skegness and Clacton were taken over for military use. The Admiralty asked Billy Butlin to build two more camps for them to be used by military personnel. These were constructed at Ayr in Scotland and at Pwllheli in Wales. Butlin deliberately built the camps to a design which would make it relatively easy to convert them into holiday resorts after the war. In 1946 when the war was over, the Navy moved out of the camp at Ayr and ownership reverted to Butlin, who quickly brought the camp up to holiday standard and opened it to the public the following year. When it opened, it could accommodate 2,000 visitors, but this later increased to over 5,000. The camp at Pwllheli opened in March 1947 and could eventually accommodate a total of 8,000 guests. Butlin went on to open a camp at Mosney in Ireland in 1948. Three more camps opened in the 1960s and these included one at Bognor Regis in

1960, another at Minehead in 1962 and finally one at Barry Island in 1966.

Mums who toiled at home were well looked after at Butlin's and, for a change, had their meals cooked for them. The camps proved hugely successful and many families returned year after year. Children enjoyed the funfair rides, including the dodgems; took part in the many competitions; joined the Beaver Club and enjoyed roller skating and boating.

A trip to Butlin's would be all a kid would talk about when he came back from holiday. Other children would want to hear all the details and be envious of the fun, the rides and the entertainment to be had there, and no doubt then went straight back to their parents to hassle them to take them there.

Many children would never be taken anywhere as exciting as Butlin's and would have to make do with the occasional 6*d* Woolworths day trip on the train. Many kids were lucky living relatively close to the seaside, but children in big cities might never get to see either the countryside or the sea. To them, any holiday somewhere different was a great adventure that would be talked about for weeks after.

The first package holidays abroad started in the early 1950s, but these were for the very rich and the average person could only dream of taking such a holiday. It would be another twenty years before foreign travel would become commonplace.

School holidays were looked on with much anticipation, especially the long, seemingly never-ending summer holidays, when the best weather of the year and the longest days made it an ideal time to get out and play, explore and generally have an adventure. Even children who weren't taken away on holiday always had plenty to tell their classmates when they returned to school after the break. The summer would have been filled with fun, exploring, building dens, building go-karts, and playing Cowboys and Indians, together with other mock battles. There was always a boy in class who came back looking worse for wear because he'd fallen off a wall or out of a go-kart or something similar. Children were more adventurous in the 1950s and would try anything, from making their own parachutes and jumping off walls on bomb sites (sometimes with disastrous results) to attacking each other with home-made swords or guns as they relived some of the action they'd seen in films at the cinema or on television. Every boy wanted to be Robin Hood, Roy Rogers or Ivanhoe, and it all made the long hot summers one big adventure. Perhaps girls didn't feel the same, as boys interrupted games of hopscotch and skipping to play football or war games. Returning to school after the summer break would seem very boring to most kids, and many would be itching to get out of the classroom as soon as possible before the dark nights of winter set in.

The Christmas holiday would also be much anticipated. Although much shorter than the summer holiday, there was much to look forward to, including new toys which would soon be shown off to all their friends.

All in all, people were happy with their lot, taking holidays occasionally to the seaside, walking along the pier eating candy floss or ice cream or having picnics out in the country.

15

Technology

Amazingly, colour television, remote controls, the credit card, superglue, black box flight recorders, the hovercraft, liquid paper, video tape recorders, the transistor radio, music synthesisers, Teflon pans, fibre optics, the first computer hard disk, the modem, the pacemaker, microchips and the laser were all inventions of the 1950s. However, many seem to have taken a while to make their way to British shores. Many families in the UK wouldn't own a colour television until the 1970s and remote controls wouldn't arrive until the 1980s. Hard drives, modems, fibre optics, etc., all seem a lot more recent to us.

In 1950, Ralph Schneider invented the first credit card or 'Diners' card. A form of credit card had been around since the 1920s in America, but the 'Diners' card paved the way for all future credit cards. In 1958, American Express issued their very first credit card although it was a very long way into the future before they became commonplace in Britain.

Colour televisions were first on sale in America in 1953, although it would be more than twenty years before they would become commonplace in the UK. Colour broadcasts in Britain didn't start until 1967.

In the 1950s, in Britain, most people were happy if they had a black and white set and, perhaps, a Kenwood mixer for the kitchen!

The first microchip was developed in 1959 and changed technology forever.

Cars were a relatively new thing to most families and were pretty basic compared to the models of today. A car wouldn't be fitted with a radio and even things like automatic windscreen wipers could be a novelty.

Technology advanced quite a way in the 1950s. The first satellite, Sputnik, was launched in 1957, and started the space age and the space race between the Soviet Union and America, which ultimately ended up with America putting a man on the moon.

In the home, there were more compact record players and 45 rpm discs instead of 78 rpm shellac records. Other technology included the invention of the first leak-free ballpoint pen, the first copy machine and the invention of Polypropylene. In America, the first car to have a fibreglass body (the Chevrolet Corvette) was produced in 1953. Bell Telephone labs produced the first solar battery in 1954 and a solar-powered wristwatch was invented in 1956.

Most people living in Great Britain in the 1950s were little affected by modern technology. Television sets were the latest must-have appliance, and technology advanced slowly for most people, although much of the new technology available did affect home life, with the inventions of new kitchen appliances, hoovers, washing machines, fridges, etc.

16

Cars and Transport

Motor fuel rationing came to an end on 26 May 1950. Amazingly, before the war, the small narrow streets of many towns and cities had become congested with traffic. Policemen would be put on patrol at busy junctions to guide the traffic safely through. The heavy bombing during the war meant that, when they were rebuilt, the streets were wider for easier accommodation of traffic. However, most families at the beginning of the 1950s didn't own a car, and much of the heavy traffic during the war years came from buses, work vans and lorries, trams, and cars owned by the middle classes.

It wasn't unusual to see a street empty of cars in the 1950s. There were no parking problems, and backstreets were empty enough for kids to play football or other games with little fear of being knocked down or injured. Many roads were still cobbled, and the only transport would be a delivery van delivering goods to the local grocers, the milkman, the ice cream man, the postman on his bicycle, or perhaps a rag-and-bone man complete with horse and cart. Backstreets were very quiet places for vehicles, and children could be seen happily playing up and down them while their mothers watched, happily talking to their neighbours.

Cities were busier places, with bustling traffic including buses, cars and work vehicles. Even so, it was nothing like the stream of steady traffic of today.

In 1950, 1 in 7 people owned a car in the UK, but there were still many new models around. Ford produced several popular models including the Anglia, the Prefect and the Popular. The Popular was produced between 1953 and 1962, and when it was first manufactured it was Britain's cheapest car.

The Anglia and the Prefect stopped being produced in 1953, and the Popular succeeded them. Over 150,000 Populars were produced, and it was successful because of its lower cost – around £390. Even so, a car was still out of reach for most families. In 1959, the old Popular was replaced with a new version of the car, which included a sleeker, more modern Anglia body.

Other popular cars of the 1950s included the Mark I Ford Consul and Zephyr models, which were first on show at the Earl's Court motor show in 1950. Production of the Consul began in 1951. The Mark I model was produced until 1956, when the Mark II Consul, Zephyr and Zodiac went on sale. The three cars were known as the Three Graces. The Mark II range proved to be a huge seller.

The British Motor Corporation Limited was formed in early 1952 on the merger of Austin and Morris. The BMC operated from Longbridge in Birmingham. In its day, BMC was the largest British car producer. In 1952, it manufactured 39 per cent of all cars sold in Britain. It produced a wide selection of cars under the brand names Austin, Morris, MG, Austin-Healey and Wolseley. One of their most popular cars was the Mini, which was produced from 1959 onwards. It was designed for BMC by Sir Alec Issigonis and manufactured at the Longbridge and Cowley plants. In 1958, BMC employed Battista Farina, an Italian automobile designer, to redesign its whole car line. The first car produced was the Austin A40 Farina, which rolled off the production line in the same year. The Countryman version combined the qualities of a saloon and a hatchback, giving more passenger room and luggage space. The Wolseley 15/60 also rolled off the production line in December 1958. It was a mid-sized car with sleek lines. Other cars that appeared shortly after included the Riley 4/68, Austin A55 Cambridge Mark II, MG Magnette Mark III and the Morris Oxford V.

As the decade advanced, more and more families owned their own car, but backstreets were still quite empty of traffic.

In the 1950s, the government gave the go-ahead for Britain's first motorways to be built. In 1958, the first section of motorway opened was the Preston Bypass in Lancashire. In 1959, the M1 became Britain's first full-length motorway. Documentary film of the day shows very little traffic on these first motorways and it's hard to imagine that the land's roads were ever that quiet.

Busy streets led to a passion among boys – collecting car number plates! Writing down as many number plates as you could was all a boy needed to occupy himself for a day. It's amazing nowadays that children were once so easily amused. I-Spy books connected with traffic were also very popular, and included 'I-Spy on the Road', which had kids spotting various road signs and vehicles. Other books included 'I-Spy Transport' and, of course, 'I-Spy Cars'. They were ideal for long journeys, where kids in the back of the car could spot as much as possible along the way.

A car was still a luxury by the end of the 1950s, but by then many people now owned their own. As the roads and towns became busier with traffic, the first parking meters were installed on 10 July 1958.

A car journey for a child was an adventure. Trips to the seaside and visits to relatives or friends had previously been taken by train or bus, but as the 1950s marched on more and more families owned their own car.

A British car won Le Mans in 1959. Carroll Shelby, an American, co-drove an Aston Martin DBR1, together with Englishman Roy Salvadori, to race to victory, beating France's

Maurice Trintignant and Belgium's Paul Frère, who were also driving an Aston Martin DBR1. Ferrari came third.

For people who didn't have cars, and many didn't, the only other way to get anywhere by vehicle was on a double-decker bus. In the 1950s, all buses had conductors, who would take your money – it would have to be change because they wouldn't accept notes – and issue you with a small ticket. Children loved bus tickets and would hassle the driver or conductor for a roll of them. Some kids collected them.

1950s police cars were mainly small vehicles, including the Austin A70 and later the A90. Sergeants and inspectors drove Hillman Minxes, and Hillman Huskies were used as general vehicles. Morris Commers were used to transport prisoners and personnel. Motorbike cops used Triumph 5T 500cc and 350s, complete with radios fitted in about 1956. Most motorbikes used were either Triumphs or Nortons. The bikes had a large box on the back to carry all the equipment needed to send and receive radio messages. Many policemen still had pushbikes and called in crimes in one of the many blue police phone boxes. The Ford Anglia and Ford Popular became well-used police cars towards the end of the decade.

Children were fascinated by police cars and fire engines and the 'nee-nah' sound they later made. Earlier police cars had distinctive bells called Winkworth Gongs.

There was one other vehicle that all kids of the 1950s loved, and that was the ice cream van with its distinct tunes. Wherever one stopped, a queue was sure to form. The chimes of the van signalled that summer was here, together with warm weather and long school holidays. Ice cream was served hard, scooped or as soft ice cream. The sound of an ice cream chime instantly takes you back to childhood and summer whether it's playing 'Greensleeves', 'Popeye the Sailorman', 'Whistle While You Work' or 'You are my Sunshine'.

The cost of a new Mini in 1959 was approximately £496, which would have taken an average worker about a year to earn.

17

Events

1950:

Listen with Mother
On 16 January, the BBC Light programme began to broadcast the children's programme *Listen with Mother*. It was presented by Daphne Oxenford and featured stories, songs and nursery rhymes.

Clement Attlee
Clement Attlee won the general election on 24 March taking Labour into a second term of government. However, he lost many seats, including one to a thirty-three-year-old Conservative candidate, Edward Heath, who would later become Prime Minister himself.

'The Gambols'
The comic strip 'The Gambols' first appeared in the *Daily Express* on 16 March. The strip was created by Barry Appleby and has run ever since. It features two central characters, George and Gaye Gambol, a suburban, middle-class couple.

Eagle
On 14 April, the comic *Eagle* was first published. It included strips featuring Dan Dare and Captain Pugwash. It ran until

1969 and was relaunched in 1982. It was the brainchild of Marcus Morris, who was an Anglican vicar from Lancashire. The strips were drawn by Frank Hampson.

The Grand Prix

The first World Championship Formula One Grand Prix was held at Silverstone on 13 May. The race, which was contested over seventy laps, was won by Giuseppe Farina, who was driving for the Alfa Romeo team. Luigi Fagioli finished second (also in an Alfa Romeo) and Englishman Reg Parnell finished third.

Holiday Travel

Vladimir Raitz of Horizon Holidays organised the first package holiday air charter overseas. The camping trip travelled from Gatwick to Corsica.

Fuel Rationing

After eleven years, motor fuel rationing came to an end on 26 May. However, at the time, many people still did not have cars. Long queues appeared at garages as rationing ended, and many people happily tore their ration books up into confetti. Philip Noel-Baker, the Minister for Fuel and Power, announced that two American companies had made a pact to supply oil in return for buying British goods.

Educating Archie

On 6 June, *Educating Archie* was first broadcast on the BBC Light Programme. The show featured Max Bygraves, together with ventriloquist Peter Brough and his dummy, Archie Andrews. The programme attracted over 15 million listeners and had a fan club of 250,000.

The Archers

The Archers was first broadcast on 7 June on BBC Radio. It was billed as 'an everyday story of country folk' and was soon attracting millions of listeners. At its height, it was estimated that 60 per cent of people living in the British Isles were regular listeners.

Andy Pandy

The children's favourite throughout the 1950s and 1960s, *Andy Pandy* was first broadcast on BBC on 11 July. It featured a marionette who lived in a picnic basket and was joined by Teddy and Looby Loo, a rag doll. The show was narrated by Maria Bird and became immensely popular with small children.

The England Football Team

The English national football team competed in the World Cup for the first time in Brazil on 24 June. British teams had withdrawn from FIFA in 1920 because they refused to play teams that they had previously been at war with. The winners of the World Cup that year were Uruguay, who beat Brazil 2-1.

Sainsbury's

In Croydon, Sainsbury's opened its first self-service supermarket on 31 July. Sainsbury's had been trading since 1869 and became Great Britain's largest grocery group in 1922.

Princess Anne

Princess Anne was born to Princess Elizabeth and the Duke of Edinburgh on 15 August. At the time, she was third in line to the throne (after her brother Charles) and would be second in line when her mother became queen. However, today, she is tenth in line. Over the years, she has become best known for her endless charitable work, and carries out 500 royal engagements a year.

The First Broadcast from Europe
On 27 August, the first BBC live broadcast was transmitted from the European continent. The one-hour television special was introduced by Richard Dimbleby and included live pictures of the Hôtel de Ville in Calais as well as civic celebration and entertainment.

1951:

World's First Commercially Available Computer
In February, the world's first commercially available computer was delivered to the University of Manchester by Ferranti. The machine was designed at the University of Manchester by Freddie Williams and Tom Kilburn.

Dennis the Menace
Dennis the Menace, one of Britain's best-loved comic-strip characters, first appeared in *The Beano* during March. It told the story of a badly behaved schoolboy, who was accompanied in his adventures by Gnasher, his Abyssinian wire-haired tripe hound. On 14 September 1974, Dennis the Menace replaced Biffo the Bear on the front cover of *Beano*.

The Festival of Britain
George VI opened the Festival of Britain on 3 May. The event was held in the summer of 1951 and was used by the government to show people how Britain was recovering after the Second World War. The centrepiece was located on the South Bank of the Thames, but there were also events in Poplar for architecture, South

Kensington for science, Battersea for the Festival Pleasure Gardens and Glasgow for Industrial Power. There were further celebrations in Cardiff, Bath, Bournemouth, Perth, Stratford-upon-Avon, York, Aldeburgh, Inverness, Cheltenham and Oxford, as well as many other places.

The Goon Show

On 28 May, *The Goon Show* was first broadcast on BBC radio. It featured Spike Milligan, Harry Secombe, Peter Sellers and Michael Bentine. The first series was entitled *Crazy People*, but it was renamed *The Goon Show* thereafter. Spike Milligan was the main creator and writer of the show, which featured surreal humour, puns, catchphrases, comical voices and bizarre sound effects.

The Exhibition of Industrial Power

Princess Elizabeth opened The Exhibition of Industrial Power in Glasgow on 28 May as part of the Festival of Britain. The exhibition told the story of industrial power and showcased new technology, as well as telling the story of energy and science. Princess Elizabeth, in her opening speech, announced that she was a lover of Scotland and said the exhibition 'was a well-deserved compliment to the land of so many famous engineers and inventors'.

1952:

The Death of George VI

On 6 February, George VI died, aged 56, after a long illness. He was succeeded by his daughter, Princess Elizabeth, who, at the time of his death, was on holiday in Kenya with the Duke of Edinburgh.

The Neo-Edwardians, Teddy Boys or Teds Were Seen Around London

Teddy boys were inspired by the dandies of the Edwardian age, wearing styles introduced by Savile Row tailors after the war. The subculture of Teddy boys started in London and soon spread across Great Britain, quickly becoming associated with the new rock 'n' roll scene.

The Lynmouth Floods

On 16 August, Lynmouth was devastated by floods, which left thirty-four people dead. Approximately 100 buildings were destroyed or badly damaged, and twenty-eight of the thirty-one bridges were washed out to sea. Over 420 people were made homeless in the floods.

Winston Churchill Became Prime Minister

Winston Churchill started his second spell as Prime Minister of Great Britain on 26 October 1951. He remained in office until 7 April 1955. He had previously been Prime Minister between 10 May 1940 and 26 July 1945.

The Great Smog

On 4 December, a killer fog descended on London. The Great Smog of 1952 was also known as the Big Smoke. A spell of cold weather, together with an anticyclone and still conditions, collected airborne pollutants, particularly from the use of coal, which formed a thick layer of smog over the city. In total, it lasted from Friday 5 to Tuesday 9 December 1952, and dispersed quickly after a change in the weather. Medical reports stated in the weeks following that an estimated 4,000 people had died prematurely, and a further 100,000 became ill because of breathing problems caused by the smog. Recent research shows that the number of fatalities was far greater, at about 12,000.

1953:

The Queen's Coronation

The queen's coronation gripped a nation. It was the one event that resulted in many homes having their first television set. Princess Elizabeth's father, King George VI, died on 6 February 1952. The coronation of Queen Elizabeth took place on 2 June 1953 and was watched by millions. It was the first coronation to be televised, and also the first major event to be broadcast on television. There was much debate about the ceremony being filmed before television cameras, and Winston Churchill was against the idea. However, it was broadcast live to millions of viewers all over Great Britain. Although broadcast in black and white, the ceremony was also filmed in colour and experimental 3D. So that the film could be seen in Canada the same day, it was flown over by RAF Canberras and was later transmitted by the Canadian Broadcasting Corporation.

Mount Everest Conquered

Edmund Hillary and his Nepalese Sherpa Tenzing Norgay conquered Mount Everest on 29 May 1953. They were taking part in a ninth British expedition led by John Hunt. Two climbing pairs were selected by Hunt to try and conquer the summit. The first pair, which included Tom Bourdillon and Charles Evans, came within 100 metres of the summit on 26 May but turned back after suffering from oxygen problems. The second pair, Edmund Hillary and Tenzing Norgay, reached the summit at 11.30 a.m. local time on 29 May using the South Col Route.

1954:

Rationing Ended in 1954

Housewives celebrated as fourteen years of food rationing ended at midnight on 4 July, when restrictions on the sale of meat and bacon were lifted. A special ceremony was held at Trafalgar Square in London by members of the London Housewives' Association. For the first time, London's Smithfield Market opened at midnight instead of 6 a.m., and meat sellers had a job keeping up with all the trade.

Roger Bannister Broke the Four-Minute Mile

Roger Bannister broke the four-minute mile on 6 May. At the time, he was a twenty-five-year-old medical student. Watched by 3,000 spectators, he achieved a time of 3 minutes 59.4 seconds at the track at Iffley Road, Oxford. He had once been the president of the Oxford Club, and was competing against his old university while running for the Amateur Athletic Association. He was aided by two pacemakers, Chris Brasher and Chris Chataway. When he was just 200 yards from the finishing line, Bannister sprinted in record time, before falling exhausted into the arms of the Reverend Nicholas Stacey. There was huge excitement when the crowd of spectators realised that he had broken the world record. Bannister retired from running at the end of 1954 to pursue his medical career. He later became a consultant neurologist. He was knighted in 1975.

1955:

Sutton Coldfield Rail Crash

On 23 January, a train crash at Sutton Coldfield left seventeen people dead and forty-three injured when an express train took a curve too fast and derailed. Following the incident, speed restriction signs by the lineside were universally adopted. Before this, there were no visual signs reminding the driver of the speed restrictions on many routes.

The Big Freeze
On 24 February, a cold spell hit Great Britain, which resulted in seventy roads being blocked with snow. In some isolated areas, the Royal Air Force had to deliver food. Hundreds of vehicles were abandoned as snow drifts reached 30 feet. Temperatures fell beneath -3 °C, which was the lowest temperature for thirty years. Scotland and the North were particularly badly hit, and Caithness was without power or light for several days.

Resignation of Winston Churchill
On 5 April, Winston Churchill retired due to ill health at the age of eighty. Buckingham Palace released a statement announcing the news. The statement read, 'The Right Honorable Sir Winston Churchill had an audience with the Queen this evening and tendered his resignation as Prime Minister and First Lord of the Treasury, which Her Majesty was graciously pleased to accept.' Tributes to Winston Churchill and his premiership poured in from around the world.

The Polio Vaccine
On 5 May, American Dr Jonas Salk promoted his polio vaccine in Great Britain while touring the country. Margaret Jenkins became the 500,000th person in London to receive the polio vaccine. She had decided to have the injection because two of her friends had fallen victim to the crippling effects of contracting polio. Salk was in the country for a congress of the Royal Society for the Promotion of Health.

Ruth Ellis

On 13 July, Ruth Ellis became the last woman to be hanged in Great Britain. She had been found guilty of murdering her lover, David Blakely, a twenty-five-year-old racing driver. She had shot him outside the Magdala public house in North London on Easter Sunday. There were appeals to reprieve her but these were rejected by the Home Secretary Major Lloyd George. The governor at Holloway prison had to call in reinforcements after 500 people gathered at its gates. A petition containing thousands of signatures had been collected asking for the death penalty to be lifted. The jury took just fourteen minutes to find her guilty.

1956:

Premium Bonds Introduced

Premium Bonds were first introduced in the Budget of 1956 by Harold MacMillan and offered buyers the chance to win monthly prizes. They were hugely popular with the general public who dreamed of getting rich in the same way that they dreamed of winning the football pools. The draw was introduced at the end of 1956 and numbers were picked out randomly by Ernie, which stood for Electric Random Number Indicating Equipment. The first Ernie was built at the Post Office Research Station and the machine randomly generated numbers.

Alderman Sir Cuthbert Ackroyd (later the Lord Mayor of London) bought the first Premium Bond on 1 November 1956. Over £5 million worth of Premium Bonds were bought on their first day of release. The first draw took place on Saturday 1 June 1957, by which time over £82 million had been invested. The draw was held at the Premium Bonds headquarters at Lytham St Annes in Lancashire. Altogether, there were 23,000 prizes in the first draw, with the top prize being £1,000, which seemed a fortune in those days. Prizes were announced by celebrities of the day, including Bruce Forsyth and Bob Hope.

1957:

The First Televised April Fool Joke Appeared on the BBC

The BBC broadcast the first televised April Fool's joke on 1 April 1957. The prank showed spaghetti being harvested in Switzerland. People in the 1950s were a lot more naive than they are today and many actually believed that spaghetti was grown on trees.

Harold Macmillan Made His Best-Remembered Speech

On 20 July, Harold Macmillan optimistically announced to his fellow party members at Bedford that 'most of our people have never had it so good'. The phrase is often misquoted as 'Britain has never had it so good' and is regularly repeated by modern-day politicians.

The First Appearance of Andy Capp

The cartoon featuring Andy Capp first appeared in northern copies of the *Daily Mirror* on 5 August. The cartoon was created by Reg Smythe (1917–1998). Andy Capp was a working-class character whose hobbies included darts, pigeon racing, football and snooker. Other characters featured in the strip included Flo Capp (his long-suffering wife) together with their neighbours and friends, Chalkie and Ruby White.

The Televising of the Royal Christmas Message
The queen broadcast the first ever royal Christmas message on television, in which she actually appeared, on 25 December. The queen had previously made her first radio Christmas speech in 1952.

1958:

Manchester United FC's Plane Crashed
On 6 February, the plane carrying the Manchester United team, returning from the European Cup in Belgrade, crashed on take-off at Munich Airport. A total of twenty-one of the forty-four people on the plane were killed, including seven Manchester United players.

Sir Vivian Fuchs Crossed the Antarctic
On 2 March, Sir Vivian Fuchs led the first team across the Antarctic using snowcat and dogsled teams. The journey took the British team a total of ninety-nine days. Fuchs was knighted by Queen Elizabeth II in 1958.

Work Began on the M1
On 24 March, the construction of the first stretch of the M1 began. The road, which was due to be opened in 1959, would eventually stretch from London to the Warwickshire-Northamptonshire border. Today, the motorway stretches a total of 193 miles, with most of the road being completed and opened between 1959 and 1968.

The Cod War
On 1 September, the first Cod War between Great Britain and Iceland began. They became known as the Icelandic Cod Wars, and the feud concerned the fishing rights in the

North Atlantic. The Royal Navy deployed warships and tugboats to stop the harassment of British crews. This led to confrontations between Icelandic patrol vessels and British warships, which included many incidents of ramming.

Blue Peter

Blue Peter was first broadcast on British television on 16 October and became the world's longest-running children's television show. Christopher Trace and Leila Williams were the first presenters. Trace stayed with the show for nine years and Williams presented for three.

1959:

Juke Box Jury

On 1 June, David Jacob hosted the first edition of the BBC's new programme, *Juke Box Jury*. The show ran from 1 June 1959 until December 1967. By 1962, the show was attracting 12 million viewers every Saturday night.

Postcodes

On 28 July, the Post Office introduced postcodes in Great Britain for the first time. They were introduced to improve efficiency.

The Mini

On 26 August, the first Mini went on sale. The car was made by the British Motor Corporation. The car was designed by Sir Alec Issigonis and was manufactured at the Longbridge and Cowley plants. In 1968, British Leyland took over production of the car.

The Auchengeich Mining Disaster
On 18 September, forty-seven miners died at the mine at
Auchengeich, Lanarkshire, due to an underground fire. The
fire was caused by a faulty fan used to purify the air in the
mine. The mine was eventually flooded to put out the fire.
It was one of the worst mining accidents of the twentieth
century.

18

World Events

1950:

The First Organ Transplant Took Place

On 17 June 1950, the first organ transplant took place in America. Ruth Tucker, who was aged forty-four, received a kidney at the Little Company of Mary hospital in Illinois. The kidney was rejected after ten months because there were no anti-rejection drugs or immunosuppressive therapy at the time. Tucker's remaining kidney had time to recover during the ten months and she lived for a further five years. The first successful kidney transplant took place in 1954.

The World Population Numbers Rose to 2.52 Billion

The population numbers reached 1 billion in 1804, and it was another 123 years, in 1927, before they reached 2 billion. By 1960, there were 3 billion people living in the world. Today, there are approximately 7 billion people, and forecasts for 2046 say that there will be an incredible 19 billion.

War in Korea

The Korean War began on 25 June 1950 and ended on 27 July 1953. With the fall of Japan at the end of the war, Korea was split into two halves, with Communist

Russia occupying the north and America occupying the south. The failure of free elections in the north led to the 38th Parallel, a political border between the two halves of Korea. The North Korean forces invaded South Korea on 25 June 1950, which ultimately led to military intervention in Korea.

1951:

Cleveland Disc Jockey Alan Freed Coined the Phrase 'Rock 'n' Roll'

Alan Freed is credited with coining the phrase 'rock 'n' roll', which he used to describe the uptempo black R&B records that he played from 1951 onwards on the Cleveland radio station WJW. Freed nicknamed himself the 'Moondog' and his show was listed as the 'Moondog Rock 'n' Roll Party'.

The Beauty Contest Miss World Commenced

Eric Morley created the Miss World event in 1951, and over the years it has become one of the most publicised beauty contests around the world. The first winner of the competition was Kiki Håkansson of Sweden, who was crowned Miss World 1951. Her reign proved to be the longest, lasting a total of 475 days. May Louise Flodin, also of Sweden, won the contest in 1952.

1952:

Dwight Eisenhower Elected President of the USA

Eisenhower preceded Harry S. Truman, and served in office from 20 January 1953 to 20 January 1961. While in office, he presided over the end of the Korean War, using nuclear threats, and deposed the leader of Iran in 1953.

First Mechanical Heart
On 6 February, a mechanical heart was used for the first time on a patient in America.

The Scrapping of ID Cards
On 20 February, Winston Churchill scrapped compulsory national identity cards in Great Britain. From the outbreak of the Second World War in 1939, every civilian, including children, was compelled to carry an ID card.

The Death of Eva Perón
Eva Perón, the spiritual leader of Argentina, died aged thirty-three on 26 July. She became the First Lady of Argentina on 4 June 1946 when her husband Juan Perón was elected President. He remained in office until 1955 before being re-elected in 1973.

Polio Deaths
Nearly 58,000 cases of polio were reported in America, leading to 3,145 deaths and 21,269 left with disabling paralysis.

1953:

Peter Pan
Walt Disney's feature film *Peter Pan* premiered on 5 March. The film was a huge success and was the highest-grossing film of 1953. Because of its incredible success, it was regularly rereleased in cinemas over the years until 1989, with the aim to attract new audiences of children.

A New Regime Took Over in Russia When Stalin Died
Joseph Stalin died, after years of oppression, on 5 March 1953 and was succeeded in office by Nikita Khrushchev. Stalin ruled the country between 3 April 1922 and 16 October 1952.

James Bond
On 13 April, Ian Fleming published his first James Bond novel, *Casino Royale*. A further eleven novels featuring James Bond followed. *Casino Royale* has been adapted for the screen three times, including a 1967 spoof version featuring David Niven. The story also appeared as a comic strip in the *Daily Express*.

The First Colour Television
On 30 December, the first colour television sets went on sale in America. They were priced at $1,175.

1954:

Marilyn Monroe Married
On 14 January, screen star Marilyn Monroe married the American baseball player, Joe DiMaggio. Monroe filed for divorce 274 days after their wedding.

Polio Vaccination Began
On 23 February, the first mass vaccination of children against polio started in Pittsburgh, Pennsylvania, in America.

The Hydrogen Bomb
Officials in America announced that a hydrogen bomb test had been carried out at Bikini Atoll on 1 March. Today, Bikini Atoll is listed as a World Heritage Site, but is still not safe for habitation because of radiation.

1955:

In the USA, the Civil Rights Campaign Got Underway
The protest for civil rights for African American citizens to
end discrimination began in 1955 with a series of protests
and civil disobedience. Acts of civil disobedience included
the successful Montgomery Bus Boycott in Alabama (1955–
56) and various sit-ins such as the Greensboro sit-in, which
led to a Woolworths store changing its policy on racial
discrimination.

Bill Haley's 'Rock Around the Clock' Rocked the
World
'Rock Around the Clock' took the world by storm as Bill
Haley and his Comets shot to number one in the charts. A
tour of Great Britain saw seats ripped up in music halls,
leading to condemnation of rock 'n' roll. Haley had several
follow-up hits including 'Shake, Rattle and Roll' and 'See
You Later, Alligator'.

Film Idol of Teenagers James Dean Died in a Car
Accident
James Dean, star of *Giant*, *East of Eden* and *Rebel Without
a Cause*, died when his Porsche 550 Spyder had a head-on
collision.

1956:

Elvis Presley Released 'Heartbreak Hotel'
RCA released Elvis Presley's 'Heartbreak Hotel', which soon
went to number one in the charts. His debut album, entitled
just 'Elvis Presley', was released on 23 March, which led to
appearances on the *Milton Berle Show* and the *Ed Sullivan
Show*.

Prince Rainier III of Monaco Married Film Star Grace Kelly

Prince Rainier of Monaco married Oscar-winning actress Grace Kelly on 18 April 1956. It was the society wedding of the year and stories and photographs covering the event appeared worldwide. They went on to have three children, including Princess Caroline Louise Marguerite (born 23 January 1957), Prince Albert II (born 14 March 1958) and Princess Stephanie Marie Elisabeth (born 1 February 1965).

1957:

The Frisbee

On 13 January, the Wham-O company produced the first frisbee. The discs had been produced previously and sold since the 1930s by Walter Morrison. In 1948, they were made in plastic and renamed Flyin-Saucer to cash in on the recent spate of UFO sightings. The rights were sold to Wham-O in 1957 and the product was renamed Frisbee.

Dr Seuss

Dr Seuss' book *The Cat in the Hat* was first published on 1 March. His other books published in the 1950s included *If I Ran the Zoo* (1950), *Horton Hears a Who!* (1955), *If I Ran the Circus* (1956) and *How the Grinch Stole Christmas* (1957). He also wrote the fantasy film *The 5,000 Fingers of Dr. T*, which was released in 1953.

The First Satellite, the Russian 'Sputnik', Orbited the Earth

Sputnik was launched by the Soviet Union into orbit on 4 October 1957 and became the first artificial earth satellite. It started the space age and began the space race between

America and the Soviet Union to develop political and military technology and ultimately put a man on the moon.

1958:

De Gaulle Became President of France
Charles De Gaulle was a French general who founded the French Fifth Republic in 1958 and became its first President from 1959 to 1969. He was a veteran of the First World War and achieved the rank of Brigadier General during the Second World War. He was succeeded by Georges Pompidou.

NASA Founded
The National Aeronautics and Space Administration was established on 29 July 1958. They were responsible for the Mercury, Gemini and Apollo projects. Space travel captured people's imaginations, and their ultimate goal, landing men on the moon, was achieved eleven years later in July 1969.

Stereo LP Records First Sold
The first mass-produced stereo vinyl records were produced in 1958. In America, they were issued by Audio Fidelity and in Great Britain, they were issued by Pye. Early records included classical, folk and stage productions, but very quickly all forms of music were soon released in stereo.

1959:

Castro Took Power in Cuba and Became the New Dictator
Fidel Castro took over power from Fulgencio Batista, who had served as the elected President of Cuba between 1940

and 1944 and as a dictator between 1952 to 1959.

Castro overthrew Batista during the Cuban Revolution. Raúl Castro, Fidel's brother, took over power in 2008.

Barbie Dolls First Produced

Barbie dolls were made by the American company Mattel, and were launched in March 1959. They were based on a German toy doll called Bild Lilli. Ruth Handler developed the idea for Mattel, who renamed the doll Barbie and introduced it at the American International Toy Fair. Over a billion dolls have been sold to date.

The Microchip Was Invented, Making Way for Future Home Computers

The microchip was developed by Jack Kilby, who was employed by Texas Instruments at the time. The first customer for the newly developed microchip was the US Air Force. The microchip went on to revolutionise technology.

Mary Quant Designed Suit Shapes That Later Hallmarked the Sixties Fashion Look

During November 1955, Mary Quant, together with Plunkett-Greene and a solicitor called Archie McNair, opened a small clothes shop on the King's Road called Bazaar. Good sellers were small plastic white collars used to brighten up black dresses and T-shirts. In 1957, the trio opened a second branch of Bazaar.

Alaska and Hawaii Became States of the USA

Alaska became the forty-ninth state of America on 3 January 1959, with Hawaii becoming the fiftieth state on 21 August 1959.

19

Christmas

Christmas was a time of great excitement for children. People were more naïve then, and all children believed in Father Christmas.

As the Christmas holidays approached, there was much activity at school. Preparations for the school nativity play would be well underway. Everyone knew the story of the baby Jesus, Mary and Joseph and the Three Wise Men. The Bible played a big part in classroom teaching. Mothers of children chosen to appear in the nativity play would do their best to make costumes out of what material they had. Some would be impressive and decorated with paste jewellery, while others did their best with a towel for a headdress, a sheet and an old belt. Children would also help to make costumes and decorate the scenery. They would make the crib out of anything that was available, sometimes using an old shoebox, or something similar, and some straw, together with characters featured at the Nativity, including Mary and Joseph, Jesus, the Three Wise Men and a donkey. All would be hand-made by the children, unless a school already had pre-prepared figures from previous years. There was something wonderful about the nativity play, and it made it feel like Christmas was on its way. Parents were invited to watch. Also, children were chosen to sing in the school choir or to sing carols to parents, in the street or local church. There would be much excitement in school on the lead-up to Christmas and the atmosphere would be totally different from the rest of the year.

Popular hymns and carols sung at school at Christmas included 'O Little Town of Bethlehem', 'Away in a Manger', 'O Come All Ye Faithful', 'Silent Night', 'Hark the Herald Angels Sing' and 'Once in Royal David's City'. Other popular carols sung were 'The First Noel', 'The Holly and the Ivy', 'We Three Kings of Orient Are', 'We Wish You a Merry Christmas', 'While Shepherds Watched', 'White Christmas', 'Deck the Halls', 'Ding Dong Merrily on High', 'Jingle Bells', 'God Rest Ye Merry Gentlemen' and 'Good King Wenceslas'. Children could make a few pennies by singing carols at neighbours' doors. Lucky ones would be rewarded with sixpences or hot mince pies or sausage rolls.

The song 'Rudolph the Red-Nosed Reindeer' was very well known by the 1950s. In 1949, Gene Autry had had a huge hit with it in America, reaching the number one spot and selling over 2.5 million records in the first year. It would go on to sell over 25 million over the years. The words to the song were originally a poem featured in a book in 1939. It was given away to children who visited the American retail outlets of Montgomery Ward at Christmas.

In class, children would make colourful paper chains by cutting strips of paper, gluing the ends and linking them together. Christmas cards were also made for parents or relatives as well as cardboard stars for the top of the tree. Cards would have featured nativity scenes and fewer pictures of Father Christmas.

Christmas wasn't as commercial as it is today, although shops would decorate their windows and some would compete to see who could produce the best lights and decorations.

At the end of the term, there would be a huge party for the kids which would include snacks, jelly, cakes and any other food that mothers had made for their kids to take in. There were party hats and much excitement, perhaps even a few home-made crackers. Party games played included pass the parcel and musical chairs.

A trip to the local department store to see Father Christmas was a must. Certainly more children believed in Father Christmas back in the 1950s than they do nowadays. Father Christmas would sit the child on his knee and ask them what they wanted for Christmas. Many would have extravagant wants.

Back home, the anticipation of Christmas Day added to the excitement. Some children would have Advent calendars which commenced on 1 December, and a door would be opened until it reached the magical day. Each door would have a Christmas scene or something biblical behind it, like Mary and Joseph, the Three Wise Men or the Star of Bethlehem, etc. 25 December would feature the baby Jesus in a crib.

Decorating the tree and front room would add to the excitement and festivities.

On Christmas Eve, children would leave out a mince pie for Santa and perhaps a glass of milk for his reindeer. Children were told that Santa came down the chimney to deliver presents, and those who didn't have chimneys were told that he had a special key so he could get in.

When Christmas Day arrived, most children would be up early (before their parents) and unwrapping the presents that Santa had left in the middle of the night. Some children would have stockings at the end of their beds with their presents, while many would have them downstairs under the tree. Most boys hoped for the latest Hornby train set, while most girls longed for a doll.

At the beginning of the 1950s, sweets, meat and butter were still rationed. Christmas dinner quite often included chicken, which would be bought from the local shop. Some people kept their own chickens in the back garden. Christmas puddings would be prepared about three weeks prior to Christmas Day. Turkey was popular with roast potatoes, stuffing, Yorkshire pudding, carrots, Brussels sprouts and gravy.

After dinner, any relatives who lived nearby, including aunts and uncles, would turn up sometimes, bringing with them more gifts for the children. The afternoon was filled up with playing games until everyone was exhausted and settled down to listen to the radio or, in the later 1950s, to watch the television.

Children's television programmes for 1950 included, on 23 December, *Whirligig*, which was a fortnightly show introduced by Humphrey Lestocq and Mr Turnip. Within the programme were featured *Box of Tricks* with Geoffrey Robinson, *Flying Visit* with Marcel Stellman, and the adventure serial *Write it Yourself*, which was written by viewers and presented by Frank Coven. The programme also featured *Hank Rides Again* with Francis Coudrill.

Christmas Eve shows included, at 5 p.m., a story by Kenneth Grahame called *The Reluctant Dragon*, which starred Jeremy Spenser.

The children's television shows for Christmas Day featured *Muffin the Mule* at 5 p.m. This was followed at 5.20 p.m. by *Children's Christmas Party*, which was broadcast from the Hammersmith Palais where London's taxi drivers 'take the day off to enjoy themselves and bring happiness to the children'. Vic Oliver was the children's 'uncle' and Michael Miles hosted 'Radio Forfeits'.

The main Boxing Day show for children was *The Cruise of the Toytown Belle*, which featured Larry the Lamb played by Glenda Davies. Other characters featured included Dennis the Dachshund and Ernest the Policeman.

As many families didn't have televisions in the 1950s, the shows either went unwatched or were viewed at other people's houses.

There would be Christmas pantomimes shown on the television in the later 1950s featuring stars such as Charlie Drake, Tommy Cooper, Frankie Howerd and Spike Milligan. There were also Christmas versions of *What's My Line?* (presented by Eamonn Andrews) and the Black and White Minstrels. American imports included Harry Belafonte singing Christmas carols, as well as a host of other American stars.

Christmas was more of a family affair, with everyone coming together on the day for Christmas dinner and all that went with it.

20

Memorable Personalities of the 1950s

Gerry Anderson (14 April 1929 – 26 December 2012)
A British writer, director and producer with television shows specifically aimed at children. Many of his shows contained specially modified marionettes, for which he coined the phrase 'Supermarionation'. His first production was for ITV in 1957 and was called *The Adventures of Twizzle*. He formed the production company AP films, which would later become Century 21 Productions. He found great success in the 1960s with immensely popular children's television shows such as *Thunderbirds*, *Captain Scarlet* and *Joe 90*.

Arthur Askey (6 June 1900 – 16 November 1982)
Arthur Askey was an actor and comedian who found fame in the 1940s in films such as *Band Waggon* (1940), *The Ghost Train* (1941) and *I Thank You* (1941). By the 1950s, he was a household name appearing on television in *Before Your Very Eyes!* in 1952. In 1957, he also appeared in *Living It Up*, a sitcom based on the *Band Waggon* format, which also starred Richard Murdoch. He had many catchphrases including 'hello playmates', 'before your very eyes' and 'I thank you'. He continued to appear regularly on British television, particularly on panel shows. By the 1970s, he was a regular judge on the ITV show *New Faces*.

Clement Attlee (3 January 1883 – 8 October 1967)
Attlee was a Labour politician who served as Prime Minister between 1945 and 1951. His government undertook the nationalisation of major industries and public utilities, and also created the National Health Service. He presided over the decolonisation of much of the British Empire. Labour lost the general election in 1951 and Winston Churchill became Prime Minister. Attlee retired as leader of the party on 14 December 1955 and took a seat in the House of Lords as Earl Attlee and Viscount Prestwood. He died in 1967.

Roger Bannister (born 23 March 1929)
Roger Bannister became the first man to run a mile in under four minutes on 6 May 1954. After leaving his sporting career, Bannister became a distinguished neurologist and Master of Pembroke College, Oxford. He retired in 1993.

Michael Bentine (26 January 1922 – 26 November 1996)
Michael Bentine was a founding member of *The Goons*. After the war he became a comedian and worked at the Windmill Theatre where he met Harry Secombe. He appeared in the first thirty-eight shows of *The Goon Show* between 1951 and 1953. His first appearance on television was in *The Bumblies*, which he wrote and devised. Using puppets, the show featured three friendly aliens from the planet 'Bumble'. Throughout the 1950s, he toured Australia, and wrote scripts for Peter Sellers and for his own radio show, *Round the Bend in 30 Minutes*. He also appeared in *After Hours* with Dick Emery, and the movie *Raising a Riot* with Kenneth More. He appeared on television regularly and is fondly remembered for *Michael Bentine's Potty Time*, which ran between 1974 and 1980.

Peter Brough (26 February 1916 – 3 June 1999)

Peter Brough was a ventriloquist who appeared on radio with his talking dummy, Archie Andrews. Co-stars on the show included Dick Emery, Benny Hill, Harry Secombe, Bruce Forsyth, Tony Hancock, Hattie Jacques and Beryl Reid. Julie Andrews played Archie's girlfriend. The show was immensely popular on the radio and was transferred to BBC television in 1956 as *Where's Archie*. This was followed on ITV by *Educating Archie*. In 1961, Brough retired Archie and took over the family's textile and menswear business.

Richard Austen Butler (9 December 1902 – 8 March 1982)

Richard Austen Butler was a Conservative MP who was responsible for the Butler Education Act of 1944, which affected many children's education throughout the 1950s. In 1953, Butler acted as the head of government when Winston Churchill had a stroke. In the 1950s, he served under Churchill, Anthony Eden and Harold Macmillan, and held many positions including Deputy Prime Minister and Chancellor of the Exchequer. Butler was also the Baron Butler of Saffron Waldon. He retired from politics aged sixty-two.

Billy Butlin (29 September 1899 – 12 June 1980)

Billy Butlin was an entrepreneur who founded the Butlin's holiday camps throughout the British Isles. The first camp was opened in 1936. The camps reopened after the war, and by the 1950s were hugely successful as the destination for many British holidaymakers. One of Butlin's slogans was 'a week's holiday for a week's pay'. Billy Butlin retired in 1969, handing the business over to his son Bobby.

Max Bygraves (16 October 1922 – 31 August 2012)
Max Bygraves was an English entertainer, comedian, singer and actor. Bygraves appeared in several radio shows during the 1950s, including *Educating Archie*, and also appeared in films including *Tom Brown's Schooldays* (1951), *Charley Moon* (1956), *A Cry from the Streets* (1958) and *Bobbikins* (1959). He achieved television fame from the 1950s onwards, appearing in shows such as *Whack-O*, *The Royal Variety Performance* and *It's Sad about Eddie*. He also had his own television shows, which included *Max* (1969–74), *Singalongamax* (1978–80) and *Max Bygraves Side by Side* (1982) before hosting *Family Fortunes* (1983–85). His hit singles included 'You Need Hands', 'Tulips from Amsterdam' and 'Fings Ain't Wot They Used T'be'.

Gerald Campion (23 April 1921 – 9 July 2002)
Gerald Campion was an actor best known for his role as the overweight, greedy schoolboy, Billy Bunter. Campion played the role on television during the 1950s. By the time he had finished playing the part of Bunter, Campion was forty years old. After retiring from acting, he ran clubs and restaurants in London's Soho district. He later reprised the role of Billy Bunter in the BBC Radio 7 series *Whatever Happened to?*. By then Bunter had become Lord Bunter of Hove. Campion died in 2002.

Winston Churchill (30 November 1874 – 24 January 1965)
Prime Minster during the war years between 1940 and 1945 and again during 1951 to 1955, he is regarded as one of the greatest wartime leaders of the century and is one of Britain's most respected prime ministers. During the 1950s, he oversaw various reforms, such as the Mines and Quarries Act of 1954 and the Housing Repairs and Rent

Act of 1955. Controversially, he introduced charges for prescriptions. He will always be best remembered, though, for leading Britain during the Second World War. After a series of strokes, he died in 1965.

Jimmy Clitheroe (24 December 1921 – 6 June 1973)
Jimmy Clitheroe was a diminutive English comedian who is best remembered for playing the Clitheroe Kid on BBC Radio. He never grew taller than 4 feet 3 inches, and this made him perfect to play an eleven-year-old cheeky schoolboy. The show ran between 1957 and 1972. Even though no one saw him on the radio, he insisted on wearing a school uniform during the show. Clitheroe died of a sleeping tablet overdose aged fifty-one.

Billy Cotton (6 May 1899 – 25 March 1969)
Billy Cotton was well known as a band leader and entertainer whose band toured with ENSA during the Second World War. After the war, he appeared on the radio at Sunday lunchtimes with his show *The Billy Cotton Band Show*. The programme was broadcast between 1949 and 1968. Billy would start each show with the band's signature tune and a call of 'Wakey Wakey!' He died in 1969.

James Dean (8 February 1931 – 30 September 1955)
James Dean was an iconic American actor of the 1950s. His first appearance on television in the US was in an advert for Pepsi Cola. He also had small television and film roles before appearing in the three films which made his name. They were *Rebel Without a Cause* (1955), *East of Eden* (1955) and *Giant* (1956). His death in a car crash propelled him towards legendary status and his face still appears on posters and T-shirts worldwide.

Charlie Drake (19 June 1925 – 23 December 2006)
Charlie Drake was a popular comedian both on the radio and television from the 1950s until the 1970s. His catchphrase 'hello my darlings' was repeated in playgrounds throughout the land. His first television appearance was in *The Centre Show* in 1953. He also appeared in *Laughter in Store* (1957), *Drake's Progress* (1957) and *Charlie Drake In...* (1958–60). Many more television series followed with, perhaps, *The Worker* being his best known. Drake turned to straight acting in the 1980s and retired in 1995 after suffering a stroke.

Anthony Eden (12 June 1897 – 14 January 1977)
Anthony Eden held the office of Prime Minister between April 1955 and 10 January 1957, taking over from Winston Churchill. His reputation was damaged by the Suez Crisis. Eden resigned on 9 January 1957 due to ill health and was succeeded by Harold Macmillan.

Dick Emery (19 February 1915 – 2 January 1983)
Dick Emery was a well-known radio star during the 1950s, appearing in shows like *Chance of a Lifetime* (1952) and *Workers' Playtime*. His television debut came in *The Centre Show* in 1950 and he regularly appeared in programmes throughout the decade including *Round the Bend* (1955), *Educating Archie* (1958–59), *The Tony Hancock Show* (1956) and *Hancock's Half Hour* (1957). He then appeared regularly on television, signing a contract with the BBC to star in *The Dick Emery Show* between 1963 and 1981.

Bruce Forsyth (born 22 February 1928)
Bruce Forsyth has been appearing on British television since 1939, when he performed, singing and dancing, on the talent show, *Come and Be Televised*. Over the years, he has appeared in films including *Star!* (1969) and Disney's

Bedknobs and Broomsticks (1971). In the 1950s, he was the host of *Saturday Night at the London Palladium*. He continued to host extremely popular television shows, of which the best remembered include *The Generation Game* (1971–77 & 1990–94), *Play Your Cards Right* (1980–2003), *Bruce's Price is Right* (1995–2001) and *Strictly Come Dancing* (2004 onwards).

Alan Freed (15 December 1921 – 20 January 1965)

Alan Freed was an American disc jockey who coined the phrase 'rock 'n' roll'.

His career was destroyed by the payola scandal that hit the US in the 1960s. It was common practice for DJs to accept payments from record companies to play certain records. However, because of the scandal, Freed lost his job and no other radio station would employ him. He died aged forty-three.

Billy Fury (17 April 1940 – 28 January 1983)

Billy Fury was one of a stable of British rock 'n' roll stars produced to compete with the likes of American stars such as Elvis Presley, Buddy Holly and Jerry Lee Lewis. Fury, who was born Ronald Wycherley, had many hits including 'Halfway to Paradise' and 'Jealousy'. His hits equalled those of The Beatles in the 1960s. His heart was damaged by rheumatic fever when he was a child, and this contributed to his death; he was just forty-two.

George VI (14 December 1895 – 6 February 1952)

George VI was King of England between 1936 until his death in 1952. He was the father of our present queen, Elizabeth II (born 21 April 1926). He came to the throne on the abdication of his brother, Edward VIII. He married Lady Elizabeth Bowes-Lyon in 1923 and they had two daughters. The Second World War and heavy smoking took a toll on George VI's life and he died in 1952, aged fifty-six.

Hughie Green (2 February 1920 – 3 May 1997)
Hughie Green is fondly remembered for being the host of many game shows and the talent show *Opportunity Knocks*. He was born in London and had his own BBC radio show by the age of fourteen. He devised the show *Opportunity Knocks* in 1949 and hosted it on radio for one series before being told that it was too American for a British audience. He became a household name with the 1955 television show for ITV *Double Your Money*. The following year, *Opportunity Knocks* first appeared on television. Green died of lung cancer in 1997.

Bill Haley (6 July 1925 – 9 February 1981)
Bill Haley was born William John Clifton 'Bill' Haley, and is credited with popularising rock 'n' roll. Performing as Bill Haley and his Comets, they had hits with records including 'Rock Around the Clock', 'See You Later Alligator' and 'Shake, Rattle and Roll'. He became known as the 'Father of Rock 'n' roll' by the media and sold over 100 million records worldwide. He died in 1981 aged fifty-five in Harlingen, Texas.

Tony Hancock (12 May 1924 – 24 June 1968)
Tony Hancock was a comedian and actor best known for his shows on radio and television including *Hancock's Half Hour* and *The Tony Hancock Show*. He is best remembered for 'The Blood Donor' and 'The Radio Ham', episodes from his BBC show *Hancock*, which broadcast in 1961.

Although he was one of the best comedians of the time, he was very critical, both of himself and of his performance. He detached himself from many things that made his act so clever, including his writers Galton and Simpson and co-stars Sid James and Kenneth Williams.

Hancock took an overdose of amylo-barbitone tablets in Sydney, Australia, and died on 24 June 1968.

Sir Edmund Percival Hillary (20 July 1919 – 11 January 2008)
A New Zealand mountaineer, explorer and philanthropist who conquered Mount Everest on 29 May 1953. Following his success in reaching Mount Everest's summit, he devoted his life to helping the Sherpa people of Nepal. He was awarded the KBE in 1953. He died in New Zealand on 11 January 2008 aged eighty-eight.

Maurice Ralph Hilleman (30 August 1919 – 11 April 2005)
Maurice Ralph Hilleman was an American microbiologist who developed over three dozen vaccines, including ones for measles, mumps, hepatitis A, hepatitis B, chickenpox, meningitis, pneumonia and *Haemophilus influenzae*. His work undoubtedly saved millions of lives.

Buddy Holly (7 September 1936 – 3 February 1959)
Born Charles Hardin Holley on 7 September 1936 in Lubbock, Texan Buddy Holly had a string of hits in the late 1950s including 'Peggy Sue', and 'That'll Be the Day'. His music influenced the music of many future artists including The Beatles, The Rolling Stones and Bruce Springsteen. Holly died in a light aircraft crash in February 1959 along with Ritchie Valens and J. P. 'The Big Bopper' Richardson.

Frank Hornby (15 May 1863 – 21 September 1936)
Although not alive in the 1950s, Frank Hornby had a great influence on what every schoolboy of the 1950s desired. Hornby train sets were first produced in 1927, although the Hornby Dublo model railway system wasn't introduced until 1938, two years after he died. Hornby also invented Meccano in the early 1900s, and the ever-popular Dinky Toys.

Kenneth Horne (27 February 1907 – 14 February 1969)
A comedian who first appeared on the radio in *Much Binding in the Marsh*, which was written by his friend Richard Murdoch. He is best remembered for his two further radio shows, which included *Beyond Our Ken* (1958–64) and *Round the Horne* (1965–68). His television appearances included *What's My Line?*, *Ken's Column* and *Call My Bluff* as a team captain. He also appeared in various specials with Richard Murdoch.

David Jacobs (19 May 1926 – 2 September 2013)
An actor and broadcaster who appeared in the popular 1950s BBC radio show *Journey Into Space*. He was also a disc jockey at Radio Luxembourg and went on to present *Juke Box Jury* (1959–67) on BBC television. He also hosted the BBC's programme *Pick of the Pops* on the radio from 1955 until 1962. He's presented many television programmes over the years, including *Song for Europe* (1957–66) and *What's My Line?* which was revived in 1973.

Sid James (8 May 1913 – 26 April 1976)
An actor much-loved for his appearance in the Carry On films. He made his name as Tony Hancock's sidekick in *Hancock's Half Hour*. His first major film role was alongside Alfie Bass in *The Lavender Hill Mob* (1951). The movie also starred Alec Guinness and Stanley Holloway. He also appeared in Charlie Chaplin's *A King in New York* (1957), as well as in several other films. His success in the Carry On films led to his own television series, *Bless This House*, which was extremely popular in the 1970s.

Bill Kerr (born 10 June 1922)
During the 1950s, actor and comedian Bill Kerr played Tony Hancock's Australian lodger on the radio in *Hancock's*

Half Hour. He went on to appear in several British films including *The Dambusters* (1955) and *The Wrong Arm of the Law* (1963) before moving back to Australia. He appeared in several well-known Australian films including *Picnic at Hanging Rock* (1975), *Gallipoli* (1981) and *The Year of Living Dangerously* (1982).

C. S. Lewis (29 November 1898 – 22 November 1963)
Clive Staples Lewis was a was a novelist, poet and academic who is best known for *The Chronicles of Narnia*, the first of which, *The Lion, the Witch and the Wardrobe*, is his best-known work. His books were greatly enjoyed by children in the 1950s and have been read by millions of people all over the world.

Harold Macmillan (10 February 1894 – 29 December 1986)
Harold Macmillan was the Prime Minister of Great Britain between 10 January 1957 and 18 October 1963. He oversaw many social reforms, including the Clean Air Act (1956), the Housing Act (1957), the Offices Act (1960) and the Noise Abatement Act (1960). During his time in office, living standards rose and there was a reduction in the average working week from forty-eight hours to forty-two hours. His government was rocked by the Perfumo and Vassall scandals at the end of his reign as Prime Minister. He was succeeded by Alec Douglas-Home.

Arthur Melin (30 December 1924 – 28 June 2002) and Richard Knerr (30 June 1925 – 14 January 2008)
Arthur Melin and Richard Knerr were the inventors of the Wham-O Hula-Hoop and started a craze that spread across the world in the late 1950s. They also produced the Flyin-Saucer/Frisbee in 1958. Another popular product

included the Wham-O Superball in 1965. The company was eventually sold to Kransco Group in 1982. In 2006, Wham-O was sold for an incredible 80 million US dollars to a Chinese company, Cornerstones Overseas Investments Limited.

Spike Milligan (16 April 1918 – 27 February 2002)

A founder member of *The Goons*, Milligan was a comedian, writer and musician. He began his radio career writing material for comedian Derek Roy, before famously joining forces with Peter Sellers, Harry Secombe and Michael Bentine, performing as *The Goons*. The first show was broadcast on 28 May 1951 and became an immediate success. Milligan went on to write and appear in many other radio and television shows.

Roger Moore (born 14 October 1927)

Remembered mainly for his roles in *The Saint* and as James Bond, Moore began his television career in *Ivanhoe* (1958) and later appeared in *Maverick* (1957–62). He found worldwide fame after he was cast as Simon Templar in *The Saint* (1962–70). During the 1970s, he appeared with Tony Curtis in *The Persuaders* before taking the lead as James Bond in *Live and Let Die* (1973). He continued to play James Bond until 1985.

Jack Odell (19 March 1920 – 7 July 2007)

Jack Odell made millions of boys very happy when he invented the Matchbox range of cars and other vehicles. With Leslie Smith and Rodney Smith he formed Lesney Products. The company started in the 1950s, and by 1966 over 100 million Matchbox toys were sold every year. Odell retired in 1973 but rejoined the company when it had financial difficulties in 1981. The company was sold to Universal Toys the following year.

Jon Pertwee (7 July 1919 – 20 May 1996)

Jon Pertwee started his radio career appearing as Chief Petty Officer Pertwee in *The Navy Lark*, a show which lasted eighteen years and started in 1959. He also appeared in many films including four Carry On films: *Carry On Cleo* (1964), *Carry On Screaming* (1966), *Carry On Cowboy* (1965) and *Carry On Columbus* (1992). He appeared on television often and his most notable roles were as *Doctor Who* (1970–74) and *Worzel Gummidge* (first shown in 1979).

Elvis Presley (8 January 1935 – 16 August 1977)

Elvis Presley, 'the King of Rock 'n' roll', was born in Tupelo, Mississippi, in 1935. His many hits, including 'Heartbreak Hotel', 'All Shook Up', 'Hound Dog' and 'Blue Suede Shoes', won him fans all over the world. He caused much controversy with his hip swivelling in the 1950s, and was filmed from the waist up only on the *Ed Sullivan Show*. Presley went on to have many more hit singles in the 1960s and 1970s and appeared in many films. He died aged forty-two in 1977.

Cliff Richard (born 14 October 1940)

Born Harry Webb in 1940, Cliff Richard was considered to be the British Elvis in the late 1950s. His hit 'Move It' reached number two in the charts in 1958 and led to a career that spanned decades, with many number one hits over the years. He regularly appeared on *Oh Boy!* with other British rock 'n' rollers of the day, including Marty Wilde and Billy Fury. His other hits include 'Living Doll' (1959), 'Travellin' Light' (1959) and 'Please Don't Tease' (1960). He was knighted in 1995.

Albert Sabin (26 August 1906 – 3 March 1993)
Albert Sabin developed the first oral polio vaccine. The vaccine was easier to give to patients than the vaccine developed by Jonas Salk, and lasted longer. Sabin later developed other vaccines against viral diseases such as encephalitis and dengue. Today, it's hard to imagine the devastating effect that contracting polio had on people, and scientists like Sabin and Salk undoubtedly saved millions of lives.

Jonas Salk (28 October 1914 – 23 June 1995)
Jonas Salk was the discoverer and developer of the first polio vaccine. Polio was a dreaded illness in the 1950s and claimed the lives of many. The vaccine was introduced in 1955. Salk's sole purpose was to find a vaccine to save lives, not to make money from his discovery. It was said that, at the time, Americans' biggest fear after the atom bomb was contracting polio. In 1960, he set up the Salk Institute for Biological Studies, which, today, is a centre for medical and scientific research.

Harry Secombe (8 September 1921 – 11 April 2001)
A Welsh actor and comedian who was a member of *The Goons* and was famous for his role as Neddie Seagoon, a central character in the show between 1951 and 1960. He appeared in musicals such as *Oliver!* as well as other films. He had several hit singles including 'If I Ruled the World'. His own television show, *The Harry Secombe Show*, debuted on Christmas Day in 1968. He also hosted religious shows including *Songs of Praise* and *Highway*.

Peter Sellers (8 September 1925 – 24 July 1980)
During the 1950s, Sellers joined Spike Milligan, Harry Secombe and Michael Bentine as part of the BBC's radio show *The Goons*. He had previously made his radio debut

after the war on a programme called *ShowTime*. He also appeared in films including *I'm All Right Jack* in 1959. Later films included *Dr Strangelove* (1964), *What's New, Pussycat?* (1965), *Casino Royale* (1967) and the Inspector Clouseau Pink Panther films, which were made between 1963 and 1978. He died on 24 July 1980, aged fifty-four, after suffering a heart attack.

Jack Warner (24 October 1895 – 24 May 1981)
Jack Warner was a film and television actor who found fame and became a household name while appearing in *Dixon of Dock Green*. The show ran from 1955 until 1976 and was extremely popular with television audiences. He also appeared in many movies over the years. His last film, *Dominique*, was released in 1978. Warner died in 1981 aged eighty-five.

Marty Wilde (born 15 April 1939)
Born Reginald Smith, Wilde was discovered by impresario Larry Parnes while performing at the Condor Club in London in 1957. He was offered a recording contract, and during 1958 and 1959, he became one of Britain's leading rock 'n' roll artists, along with Tommy Steele and Cliff Richard. His hits included 'Endless Sleep', 'Sea of Love', 'Donna' and 'Bad Boy'. He regularly appeared of the television programmes *Six-Five Special*, *Oh Boy!* and *Boy Meets Girls*.

Kenneth Williams (22 February 1926 – 15 April 1988)
Kenneth Williams was a comedian, actor and writer who appeared in many radio and television shows featuring Tony Hancock and Kenneth Horne. Providing funny voices for the show, Williams found fame in *Hancock's Half Hour*. He later appeared on *Beyond Our Ken* and *Round the Horne*. He is best remembered for the many Carry On films he appeared

in during the 1960s and 1970s. He regularly appeared on television and wrote several bestselling books.

Kenneth Wood (4 October 1916 – 19 October 1997)
An entrepreneur and businessman who invented many kitchen appliances that revolutionised the kitchen in the 1950s. Best remembered for the Kenwood Chef, which was launched at the Ideal Home Show in 1950, he also produced toasters, hand mixers, liquidisers and steam irons, and soon became one of the country's youngest millionaires.

Acknowledgements

Thanks to Ellen Tait, Alan Tait, and Alan D. Tait for the photographs used. Thanks to Darrell Burge for permission to use the Hornby and Corgi adverts.

Thanks also to Tina Cole and Tilly Barker.

Please check out my website at www.derektait.co.uk.

Bibliography

Books

Kynaston, David, *Family Britain 1951–1957* (Bloomsbury, 2009).

Pressley, Alison, *The 50s and 60s: The Best of Times* (Index Books, 2007).

Tait, Derek, *An Illustrated History of Butlin's* (Amberley, 2012).

Websites

BBC News   http://www.bbc.co.uk/news.

Daily Mail   http://www.dailymail.co.uk.

Wikipedia   www.http://en.wikipedia.org.

Woolworths   http://www.woolworthsmuseum.co.uk/.

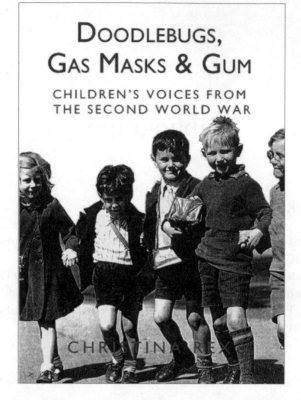